BASICS

INTERIOR ARCHITE

05

CW00957671

texture+
materials

**a
va**
academia

An AVA Book

Published by AVA Publishing SA
Rue des Fontenailles 16
Case Postale
1000 Lausanne 6
Switzerland

Tel: +41 786 005 109
Email: enquiries@avabooks.com

Distributed by Thames & Hudson (ex-North America)
181a High Holborn
London WC1V 7QX
United Kingdom

Tel: +44 20 7845 5000
Fax: +44 20 7845 5055
Email: sales@thameshudson.co.uk
www.thamesandhudson.com

Distributed in the USA & Canada by:
Ingram Publisher Services Inc.
1 Ingram Blvd.
La Vergne TN 37086
USA

Tel: +1 866 400 5351
Fax: +1 800 838 1149
Email: customer.service@ingrampublisherservices.com

English Language Support Office
AVA Publishing (UK) Ltd.

Tel: +44 1903 204 455
Email: enquiries@avabooks.com

ISBN 978-2-940411-53-5

Library of Congress Cataloging-in-Publication Data
Gagg, Russell.
Basics Interior Architecture 05:
Texture and Materials. / Russell Gagg. p. cm.
Includes bibliographical references and index.
ISBN: 9782940411535 (pbk.:alk.paper)
eISBN: 9782940447299
1.Interior architecture.
2.Interior architecture--Study and teaching.
3.Architectural design.
NA2850 .G344 2011

10 9 8 7 6 5 4 3 2 1

Design by John F McGill

Production by AVA Book Production Pte. Ltd., Singapore

Tel: +65 6334 8173
Fax: +65 6259 9830
Email: production@avabooks.com.sg

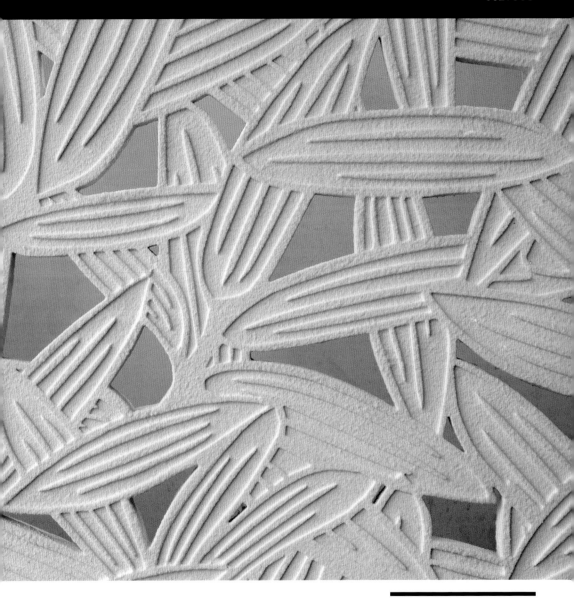

Name:
'Leafy Shade'
(see pp116+117)

Location:
Shanghai, China

Date:
2008

Designer:
A-Asterisk

Contents

Textures + Materials

Contents

This book introduces different aspects of textures and materials within the interior, via dedicated chapters for each topic. Each chapter provides clear examples from leading architectural practices, annotated to explain the reasons behind the design choices made.

Section headers
Each chapter is broken down into sub-sections, the title of which can be found at the top left-hand corner of each spread.

Section introduction
Each sub-section is introduced by a short paragraph, outlining the content to be covered.

Page numbers
Page numbers are displayed in the top right-hand corner of each spread.

Metals are ubiquitous in the construction of buildings around us. They provide the structural backbone to much of our built environment, but in doing so are often hidden beneath layers of covering and cladding. The interiors shown in this section concentrate on the qualities that metals bring to a space: texture, patination, strength and ductility. The opportunity to take on texture and ornamentation, the application of surface finishes, the ability to be bent, twisted, hammered, rolled and wrought – the inherent nature of metal – are all exemplified here.

Robert Atkinson

Name:
The Daily Express Building

Location:
London, UK

Date:
1932 (restored 2002 by John Robertson Architects)

Designer:
Robert Atkinson

Originally designed by Sir Evan Owen Williams (1890–1969), the home of the *Daily Express* newspaper was one of the finest examples of art deco design in London. With an exterior of black glass, Vitrolite panels, chromium strips at the joints and chamfered corner windows, the building presented the best of streamlined design as the expression of a modern and progressive newspaper. The interior could not have been more contrasting. Influenced by his love of cinema and the glamour of Hollywood, the Scottish architect Robert Atkinson (1883–1953) created a starburst ceiling in gold- and silver-leaf laid over plaster reliefs by Eric Aumonier depicting aspects of industry.

When combined with walls of travertine, black marble, bright metal fittings, a floor pattern of blue and black rubber outlined by narrow green strips and subtle lighting, the effect is to dazzle the visitor with the dynamism of the newspaper and the exuberance of the age.

Deane & Woodward

Name:
The Oxford University Museum

Location:
Oxford, UK

Date:
1860

Designer:
Deane & Woodward

Winning favour with the university authorities over a classical design by Barry, this neo-Gothic museum was heavily influenced by the ideas of John Ruskin in its use of materials and decoration. Designed to bring as much light into the building as possible, and making use of the production techniques of the time, the iron and glass structure originally proved too heavy and was redesigned by E A Skidmore. The resulting structure exemplifies the opportunities that the use of cast iron brought to the new museums: light, open interiors able to accommodate both the large collections that had been amassed by Victorian explorers as well as the large number of visitors that came to see them.

The opportunities that iron gave to apply decoration and fine detail were also used to allow the structure of the building to act as an expression of the purpose and aspiration of the museum. Wrought ironwork in the spandrels and at the tops of the columns represented branches of various species of tree, including sycamore, walnut and palm.

'The longer I work in this building the more I notice about it, the leaves unfurling on the pillars upstairs in the upstairs gallery, the forestry feel when you look across the museum from upstairs. It sometimes feels like it's alive and growing when you're not looking.'

Fiora Bain

Facing page :
The entrance hall by Atkinson (restored lobby by John Robertson Architects in 2002).

Above:
A Victorian-Gothic revival combination of structure and ornamentation that echoes the surroundings and context.

History and context > **International icons** > Sustainability

---

Case study information
Each case study is introduced by name, location, date and designer.

Section footers
Past, present and future sub-sections are listed in the bottom right-hand corner of each spread. The current sub-section is highlighted in bold.

Texture + Materials

The examples shown include a mix of photographs, sketches and drawings, which, when combined with detailed analysis in the text, create a unique and fascinating insight into the world of interior architecture.

Captions
All captions carry a directional and title for easy reference.

Pull quotes
Additional quotes from subject experts and practitioners.

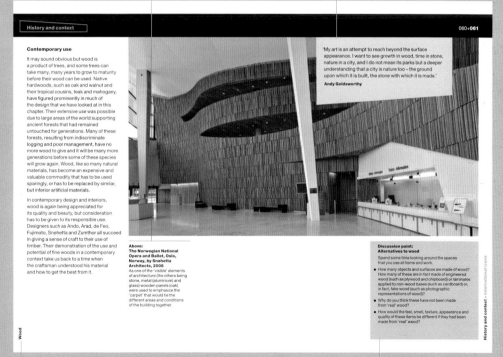

Contemporary use

It may sound obvious but wood is a product of trees, and some trees can take many, many years to grow to maturity before their wood can be used. Native hardwoods, such as oak and walnut and their tropical cousins, teak and mahogany, have figured prominently in much of the design that we have looked at in this chapter. Their extensive use was possible due to large areas of the world supporting ancient forests that had remained untouched for generations. Many of these forests, resulting from indiscriminate logging and poor management, have no more wood to give and it will be many more generations before some of these species will grow again. Wood, like so many natural materials, has become an expensive and valuable commodity that has to be used sparingly, or has to be replaced by similar, but inferior artificial materials.

In contemporary design and interiors, wood is again being appreciated for its quality and beauty, but consideration has to be given to its responsible use. Designers such as Ando, Arad, de Feo, Fujimoto, Snøhetta and Zumthor all succeed in giving a sense of craft to their use of timber. Their demonstration of the use and potential of fine woods in a contemporary context take us back to a time when the craftsman understood his material and how to get the best from it.

'My art is an attempt to reach beyond the surface appearance. I want to see growth in wood, time in stone, nature in a city, and I do not mean its parks but a deeper understanding that a city is nature too – the ground upon which it is built, the stone with which it is made.'
Andy Goldsworthy

Above:
The Norwegian National Opera and Ballet, Oslo, Norway, by Snøhetta Architects, 2008
As one of the 'visible' elements of architecture (the others being stone, metal (aluminium) and glass) wooden panels (oak) were used to emphasize the 'carpet' that would tie the different areas and conditions of the building together.

Discussion point:
Alternatives to wood
Spend some time looking around the spaces that you use at home and work.

• How many objects and surfaces are made of wood? How many of these are in fact made of engineered wood (such as plywood and chipboard) or laminates applied to non-wood bases (such as cardboard) or, in fact, fake wood (such as photographic representations of wood)?

• Why do you think these have not been made from 'real' wood?

• How would the feel, smell, texture, appearance and quality of these items be different if they had been made from 'real' wood?

Wood

History and context » International icons

Chapter footers
The current chapter is displayed in the bottom left-hand corner of each spread.

Discussion point
Additional points are raised here to promote thought, debate and discussion.

How to get the most out of this book

The choice and use of materials in interior architecture and interior design is 'endless' but the appropriate choice and correct use by the designer can have the most dramatic or the most subtle of effects. The imaginative and creative use of materials will not only satisfy the functional requirements of the space that we are designing but will also elicit the more abstract, sensual, qualities of place that we are hoping to achieve: the atmosphere. Materials might even direct or change the behaviour of those that use a space: we might feel cold or warm, excited or subdued, relaxed or anxious, all because of the 'thousand different possibilities in one material alone'.

Materials, whether they be traditional or high-tech, natural or artificial, low or high budget, form the central palette of the interior architect and designer. When working with existing spaces the success or failure of the design will often depend on the creative use of materials, their functional performance and the image, brand, identity, feel and atmosphere that they give to the space.

Materials and the textures that they either inherently possess or that can be applied to them will often define the essential qualities of a space. They are usually the first element of a design that the person comes into contact with: the handle that you grip to open a door; the wall that you brush against as you walk along a corridor; the noise that your feet make on the floor as you enter a room; the scent of the wood that surrounds you and the bright reflections from the glass that distract your eye... all of these are the result of the careful choice, treatment, positioning and assembly of materials within your design.

Name:
Switch
(see pp098+099)

Location:
Dubai, UAE

Date:
2009

Designer:
Karim Rashid Inc.

re + Materials

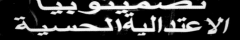

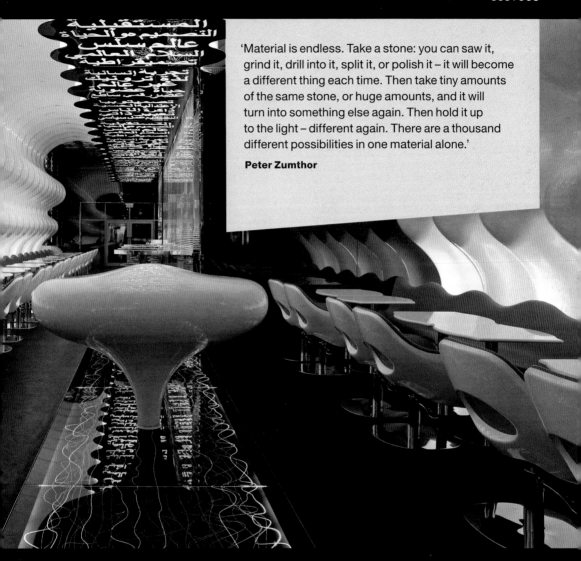

'Material is endless. Take a stone: you can saw it, grind it, drill into it, split it, or polish it – it will become a different thing each time. Then take tiny amounts of the same stone, or huge amounts, and it will turn into something else again. Then hold it up to the light – different again. There are a thousand different possibilities in one material alone.'

Peter Zumthor

To reach a point where the design of a space works, the interior architect and interior designer need to develop an intimate knowledge and familiarity with a seemingly infinite range of materials, their technical specifications and performance, construction and application techniques and their limitations, their feel, surface temperature, weight (both physical and visual), durability, their interaction with other materials, with moisture, sound and light and the potential for the application of textures and finishes. In addition, the designer should have an appreciation for the historical and cultural context of a material as well as more contemporary notions of brand, image and identity: careful selection is essential in the successful communication of a corporate message and identity.

With such a breadth of knowledge being demanded of the designer today it would be all too easy to stick with the traditional and familiar. Instead, the sheer range and variety of materials, new, old and re-invented, presents the contemporary interior architect and designer with an unparalleled opportunity for creativity, invention and expression. As technological and manufacturing processes change and develop, and the demands of clients become ever more ambitious and individual, many interior architects and interior designers are taking the opportunity to make use of materials usually found in other design disciplines. Materials used in fashion, product, transport, lighting and furniture design are being brought into play in contemporary interiors. Traditional materials, as well as those more usually found on the exterior of buildings, are enjoying a renaissance and are now often seen creating atmosphere and dynamism within spaces and buildings that have themselves been reinvented by the interior architect.

This book will provide the interior architecture and interior design student with a focused, readable and informative introduction to many of the materials currently being used in the design of contemporary interior spaces. Each chapter will identify a type of material, outline its appropriate historical context and its cultural and geographical use as well as its inherent qualities and limitations. Historic and contemporary, exemplary, case-studies will be presented in order to demonstrate where the material has been used to best effect and each chapter will raise questions regarding the sustainability of the material and its future use.

The aim of this book is not to present the student with glossy images of beautiful materials and the spaces in which they have been used but to engage the student designer in questioning where, when, how and why a material should, or could, be used. Whilst the case-studies that are presented are exemplary in the view of the author, the student should be prepared to question and critique the information presented in this book. Materials: their nature, qualities, manufacture, application and cost are constantly developing and changing as is the profession in which they are being used. In using this book, the interior architecture and interior design student should be open to change and development and the opportunities for creativity and innovation that the contemporary use of materials brings to the design of interior spaces.

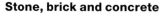

Stone, brick and concrete

Stone, brick and concrete are often referred to in architecture as being mass materials; their use being termed 'mass construction' or 'gravity construction'. These technical terms, found in architectural and construction texts, relate to the way these materials work: they rely in the simplest way on the action of gravity to keep them in place. Stone, brick and concrete work by transferring their mass, and loads applied to them, down to the ground. But these terms do little to convey the qualities that these materials bring to the spaces that use them; the skill and artistry that can be communicated in their use or the messages and atmosphere that can be created when in the hands of a skilled designer.

Name:
Jewish Museum

Location:
Berlin, Germany

Date:
1999

Designer:
Daniel Libeskind

The Jewish Museum in Berlin is testament to Daniel Libeskind's skill in crafting concrete to create expressive, monumental designs.

Stone has been used for many thousands of years in the construction of buildings. As man developed tools he began to manipulate and fashion the stones that he found around him. As society developed, so too did the skill and precision with which the stonemason worked, and the scale, opulence and grandeur of the resulting structures remain symbolic in their enduring permanence.

Facing page:
Temple of Horus,
Egypt, 57 BC
The Egyptian temples serve us well in demonstrating some of the more prominent qualities of stone. Here, the tremendous scale with which the early masons worked is exemplified by the immense column. But the care with which the stone has been crafted – rounded and carved – indicates the softer, warmer qualities of the material and demonstrates the tremendous respect the masons of the time had for the material.

Pre-history and early civilizations

The use of stone in the Neolithic house demonstrates one very important quality: permanence. The sheer effort involved in transporting, lifting, working and constructing these stone dwellings tells us that these people intended to stay put and build a community: stone signifies permanence and permanence signifies importance. But Neolithic man was not solely concerned with shelter from the harsh climate: houses were designed not only to provide shelter and safety (the most basic human requirements) but also a degree of comfort.

In the Egyptian civilization of approximately 3000 BC, the use of stone had surpassed that of western Europe. Stone was being used to its full potential. The Egyptians had realized that with big blocks of stone and careful construction you could build very big structures. The construction of temples, palaces and pyramids were all actively intended to convey the power, might, longevity and permanence of the Egyptian kingdom. The use of stone on such a grand scale emphasizes not only its permanence but the sense of monumentality that the crafting of this material brings: that a structure is of great importance intended to act as an enduring and memorable reminder.

**Above:
The Pantheon, Rome,
Italy, AD 126**
The sunlight streaming in through
the open oculus at the apex
of the roof highlights the technical
achievement of the coffered
ceiling of the dome, reducing
both the real and visual weight
of the space.

Classical civilizations

Monumentality was certainly a priority
in the ancient Greek and Roman empires.
Like great civilizations before them they
envisioned that they were going to last
forever – and they certainly built for it.
The Greeks gave us the classical orders
of architecture: Doric, Ionic and Corinthian,
still in use today. But their building was
limited to the use of the column and lintel:
the wider the span needed, the heavier
the stone lintel and the more massive the
column needed to support it. Any natural
material such as stone has an inherent
limitation in that at some point it will collapse
under its own weight.

The Romans solved this by using the
arch. The arch is made up of lots of smaller
stones called *voussoirs* that are held
tightly together by the stones to either side.
A single central stone, or keystone, is then
placed mid-point in the arch in order to push
the *voussoirs* to either side and so compress
the arch and give it its structural stability.
The use of many arches (and by extension,
vaults and domes) gives Roman architecture
a level of elegance and lightness that can
seem lacking in the earlier Greek examples.
By comparison, ancient Greek buildings,
and the spaces they contain, can seem
visually heavy and imposing.

Stone, brick and concrete

Left:
Staircase, Château de Blois,
Loire valley, France,
seventeenth century
Sumptuous carving and technical
excellence combine as the
skill of the mason and the desires
of the patron advanced into
the Renaissance.

Medieval and the Middle Ages

The ability to carve and work stone with
such precision, care and artistry was
not lost on the early Christian builders.
Armed with both skilled masons and
a desire to deliver a Christian message
across Europe, the medieval church and
state took the use of stone to, literally,
new heights. In a display of wealth and
power that has probably never been
surpassed, masons were commissioned
to ornament their buildings in the most
elaborate ways.

As European society moved into the later
Middle Ages much of the earlier built work
was seen as crude and inelegant; the term
'Gothic' was originally coined as a pejorative
term for this non-classical architecture.
However, as craftsmen were employed
to embellish these early religious buildings
with increasingly elaborate fittings in
stone, wood and metal, the term became
synonymous with richly decorated and
colourful interiors.

Discussion point:
Medieval masons

Despite often using a process of trial
and error, and given the huge logistical
obstacles that lay in their path, the skill
and audacity of the medieval mason
in successfully constructing structures
of vast volume and scale remains
largely unsurpassed.

Whilst (without the benefit of a scientific
understanding of force and materials)
many of the columns, vaults and buttresses
of medieval cathedrals may now seem
'over-designed', such clear structural
expression and rationalization has
provided inspiration to many modernist
and contemporary designers working
over a thousand years later.

● How would you describe the qualities
of the space within a medieval cathedral?

● How does the space make you feel?

● How do the qualities of the materials
used contribute to this?

● Bearing these qualities in mind, can you
think of any ways in which the work of the
medieval stonemasons might influence
an interior architect working today?

Right:
Medici Chapel, Florence, Italy, 1520–36

In the Medici Chapel, Michelangelo used symmetry and proportion to make what is overall a very grand and austere space, accessible and intimate. The large, arched niche is broken down by smaller recesses and dark banding on the floor defines an area in front of the tomb, helping the visitor to feel less exposed. Michelangelo thus removed the explicit need for physical forms of privacy, such as gates or screens, which might have been more apparent in the medieval chapel.

Facing page:
Basilica at Sant'Andrea Della Valle, Rome, Italy, 1650

With its careful use of coloured stone, stucco and gilding, as well as frescos and sculpture, the basilica at Sant'Andrea Della Valle probably ranks as one of the most outstanding examples of true rococo to be found anywhere.

Renaissance, baroque and rococo

The Renaissance brought an explosion of advances in science and art to western Europe. Such a period of stability in governance led inevitably to much greater wealth and to the demonstration of that wealth in the work commissioned from the great artists and craftsmen of the time.

Renaissance interiors were most strongly influenced by the designs of Ancient Greece and Rome, bringing together the ideas of symmetry and proportion that were being rediscovered by scholars such as Michelangelo and Leonardo da Vinci. Expensive materials such as stone, marble or brick were often used in repeated geometrical forms and patterns to give a sense of scale and proportion within classically influenced spaces. The Medici Chapel in Florence uses the inlaid patterns of the floor to connect the proportioning system of the architectural features of the space (the pilasters, arches and niches) as well as to define, break-up and give a personal scale to what might otherwise be an overwhelmingly large area.

**Discussion point:
Ornamentation**

Consider the contrast between the restrained
classicism of the Romans and Greeks and the
additional layers of ornamentation prevalent in
the baroque and rococo churches of Europe.

● Many consider these layers to have had the
effect of 'dissolving' the structure of the
building.

● How do you think ornamentation might change
the feel of a space?

History and context > International icons

'The goal was to move forward on the basis of the best human achievements of the past, while pushing ahead into an advancing future.'

John Pile

Facing page:
The Great Hall, Syon House, London, UK, Robert Adam, 1761
Stone and marble were used to great effect in the rooms commissioned by the Duke of Northumberland to create a sense of drama as well as an expression of wealth and importance.

Georgian and Regency

The elegance of the Georgian period extended into a consistency, restraint and unity of style right across architecture, interiors and their furnishings and decoration. Such an acceptable style was also easily adapted and simplified by the growing middle classes, who were offered stylish town houses, which they populated with objects and furniture by designers and craftsmen whose names still resonate with us today (Chippendale, Hepplewhite, Sheraton). Indeed, it has been suggested that such a concentration on order and consistency provided inspiration for the modernists of the early twentieth century.

Above:
The Royal Pavilion, Brighton, UK, John Nash, 1815
Chiefly an exercise in playful decoration with its mixture of oriental and Asian styles, Nash based the building around classical principles, although onion-shaped domes lend themselves to a Moorish influence rather than Roman.

As the eighteenth century moved to the nineteenth, change was the driving force, and the order of the Georgian briefly gave way to the exotic and fantastic of the Regency. The Prince Regent became George IV on the death of his father in 1820. He used his time as regent and king to experiment with design that, although rooted in the classical revival of the times, began to incorporate styles from all across the British Empire. Stylistic, architectural and cultural elements from Egyptian, Chinese and Moorish cultures, as well as knowledge from across the colonial world, were brought together in some of the most spectacular and theatrical spaces ever built.

History and context > International icons

Right:
Red House, Kent, UK,
William Morris and
Philip Webb, 1860
The rambling character of this building belies a highly rational and functional approach to the architecture that could certainly be seen as a precursor to the strict functionalism of the modernists. The Morris interiors demonstrate a lightness and simplicity that was in stark contrast to the heavy clutter of most Victorian and Edwardian domestic interiors.

Victorian

The ability to reproduce richly ornamented objects and interiors by industrial processes was not lost on a society where handmade crafts were only available to the wealthy aristocracy. Ease of production, combined with stylistic influences coming from imperial possessions in India and the Far East, allowed people to create layer upon layer of decoration and ornamentation that would often clash with reinvented architectural styles of buildings. Interiors full of vitality and energy were created, the detail and 'craftsmanship' of which has rarely been surpassed.

The aesthetic movement

The excess of the High Victorian period led to a growing reactionary movement and the search for a greater honesty in design. John Ruskin (1819–1900), a writer and theoretician, promoted the assumption that the production of art and objects by industrial means inevitably led to a vulgarity and cheapness in design that could only be countered by the craftsman. Craftsmen were considered the only group in society able to express the true honesty, meaning and purity of function through the use of materials and the production of design. Decoration and ornamentation was considered tasteless, save for that devised by the craftsman.

An aspiration towards the simple and honest became the central philosophy underpinning the movement; a realization that such an aspiration would be hard to achieve led to many of the arts and crafts designers also reinventing themselves as craftsmen in order to invent and produce the designs they wanted.

Modernism

The Bauhaus school, founded in 1919, instigated an approach to design education that ranged across architecture, interiors, printing, textiles, ceramics, lighting and furniture and took full advantage of industrial processes and modern materials. An honesty in the use of materials combined with modern methods of production came to characterize the work being produced during this period.

Given that the construction of buildings up until this point relied on heavy walls (stone, brick or concrete) to support upper floors, the large areas of glazing now appearing at the perimeter of modernist buildings seemed to defy explanation.

The opportunities afforded by the modernist use of concrete to create vast open spaces with maximum light and minimal structure are demonstrated by the spaces shown here and overleaf. They could not be more diametrically opposed in their nature, but are exemplars of how concrete was used to its maximum potential.

Below:
German Pavilion,
Barcelona, Spain, Mies
van der Rohe, 1929
Such a dramatic use of highly figured stone catches the eye and accentuates its 'mass', drawing attention from the steel columns and glass that make up much of the perimeter of the building.

Right:
798 Art Zone, Beijing,
China, 1951
This space has a distinct feel
of the Bauhaus and is a fine
example of the potential
for concrete to create open
space with minimal intervening
structure: well suited to
the demands of industrial
production.

Postmodern and contemporary

The use of mass materials today is dominated by technological developments that have concentrated around making the use of concrete, brick and, especially, stone more economical. In much of the building work we see around us, concrete or steel structural frames (traditionally perceived as being heavy) apparently defy gravity and 'float' above us. They act as a veneer, a façade, that often gives an impression of historical presence and permanence but which, in reality, is often a covering to protect the structure beneath from the weather. In the latter end of the twentieth century and the beginning of the twenty-first, one has to work hard to find examples of the use of stone, brick and concrete that still exemplify their inherent characteristics and structural opportunities.

Stone and brick are still used, albeit in more economical forms, to convey a sense of quality, permanence, monumentality and wealth – in other words for all the same reasons that they have been used throughout history. Advances in building and manufacturing technology, the movement away from dominant styles of architecture and design and the globalization of the design industry (which has removed the historic cultural connotations of material choices), have all played a part in reducing the use of traditional masonry.

Above:
Phillips Exeter Academy Library, New Hampshire, USA, Louis Kahn, 1971
In his design for the Phillips Exeter Academy Library, Kahn used 'floating' geometric shapes, cut out of reinforced concrete to create a cloistered atmosphere – appropriate, he felt, to the learning environment.

Discussion point:
Versatility

Stone is a surprisingly versatile material. It retains heat in cold weather and remains cool in hot weather. It can also be used throughout the building (floors, walls, roofs).

● Can you list other qualities that help to make stone one of the most widely used architectural materials?

We have seen that both the structural and experiential qualities of stone, brick and concrete can be fashioned and crafted in a variety of ways and using a variety of methods to create interior architecture that is infinitely more expressive and creative than we might expect. The designs that are detailed in this section exemplify the innovative use of these materials to create interiors that, whilst undeniably contemporary, owe much of their success to the generations of craftsmen that have gone before them.

Peter Zumthor

Name:
Thermal Spas at Vals

Location:
Vals, Switzerland

Date:
1996

Designer:
Peter Zumthor

The Swiss architect Peter Zumthor is considered by many to be one of the finest true craftsmen working in architecture today. The son of a carpenter, Zumthor succeeds in bringing together an intimate knowledge of materials and a profound understanding of how they work together to produce spaces that delight and seduce their users.

In his thermal baths at Vals, changes in temperature, the varying sounds of bubbling or running water, stepping down into a scented pool, the movement of the hand from cool metal to warm leather, have all been carefully orchestrated to play against the monumental backdrop of the walls of subtly textured stone (some polished, some appearing freshly quarried). Bathing becomes an immersive, emotional experience where the visitor is encouraged to linger, take time, stroll and be seduced.

Stone, brick and concrete

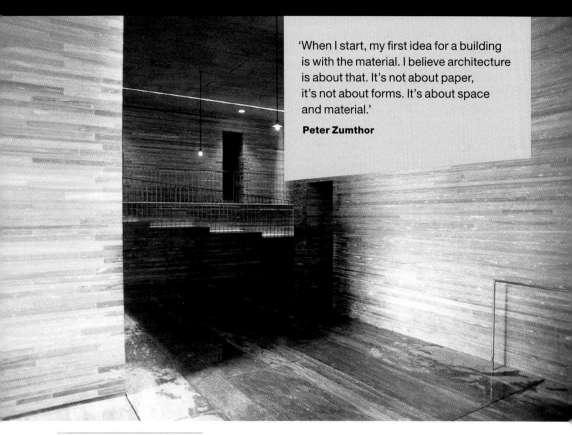

'When I start, my first idea for a building is with the material. I believe architecture is about that. It's not about paper, it's not about forms. It's about space and material.'

Peter Zumthor

Above:
Constructed out of local Valser quartzite, the rhythmic layering of stone, reminiscent of natural stone formations, produces a striking form.

Facing page:
A limited palette of materials, including chrome, brass, leather and velvet, allows the visitor to remain undistracted, focusing the attention on the space, the water and the light.

Caruso St John

Name:
The Brick House

Location:
London, UK

Date:
2005

Designer:
Caruso St John Architects

On a difficult suburban London site, overlooked on three sides and constrained by challenging planning requirements, Caruso St John Architects were asked to build a family home. Comprising concrete ceilings, glass and brick walls and floors, the simplicity of the choice of materials belies the complexity of the forms generated and the sophisticated use of the traditional opportunities afforded by bricks to provide varied patterns and textures.

Referencing a traditional London building material, the brick is given a varying, contemporary arrangement and bond as it moves the user from one space to another.

In what could be a cold and unwelcoming interior, the careful control of natural light is, instead, used to enhance the warmth of the material 'making the living areas emit a cave-like quality'. The differing surface imperfections break-up the mass of the walls giving the spaces a lightness ensuring that the house will work as a home.

Facing page:
'Like a baroque chapel in Rome buried deep within the city's close pattern of narrow streets, the expansive interior is a place of escape and dreams.'
Caruso St John

Below:
Long section of the space.

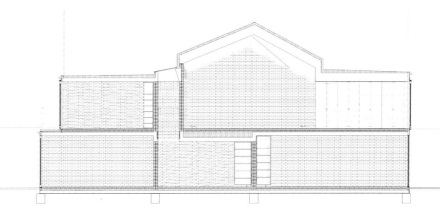

Stone, brick and concrete

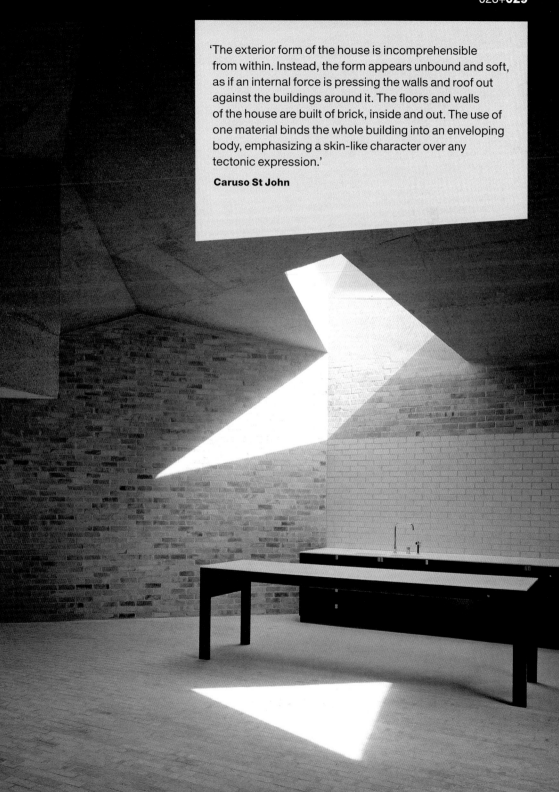

'The exterior form of the house is incomprehensible from within. Instead, the form appears unbound and soft, as if an internal force is pressing the walls and roof out against the buildings around it. The floors and walls of the house are built of brick, inside and out. The use of one material binds the whole building into an enveloping body, emphasizing a skin-like character over any tectonic expression.'

Caruso St John

Both concrete and clay-based products (brick and tile) still make up the majority of construction materials in Europe, so environmentally aware approaches to the use of these materials are of concern to both governments and the industries that have to implement policies. As the historical appreciation of these materials has shown, they are still widely perceived as essential to the construction of our built environment: they are solid and permanent, they have presence and they are known. To dismiss such long-held conventions would be unrealistic, far better to see how these materials can be used in a much more responsible way.

Permanence is an inherently sustainable quality: a building constructed of stone, brick and concrete has a much longer life than one of wood.

Stone and brick are also recyclable and reclaimable, either in their original form or as the basis for reconstituted stone or aggregates. Concrete is generally more limited in its reuse, however, and much of it can end up in landfill.

Gore Design Company of Arizona have committed themselves to a responsible, environmental approach to the use of concrete in interior fittings and finishes. By ensuring the use of water-based sealers, their products minimize the sources of volatile organic compound (VOC) pollution; pigments are free of heavy metals; recycled materials such as fly-ash are used in the construction of products to ensure that the amount of Portland cement is reduced, as is the amount of CO_2 generated.

The use of innovative products such as these allows structures to exhibit qualities synonymous with brick and stone – solidity and modular construction –without taking the same toll on the environment.

The amount of energy used in the extraction and conversion of these raw materials into useful products is again a redeeming feature: this may be justifiable in the case of stone, but the amount of energy needed in the firing of bricks or the production of cement is considerable.

Last, but by no means least, all of these products are directly or indirectly natural materials; they are of finite quantity and their extraction can cause significant environmental impact. If we accept that they form a significant and important part of the palette of textures and materials that the designer has at their disposal then we must make sure that when we use them, we do so thoughtfully and responsibly.

Stone, brick and concrete

Whatever your particular view of sustainability and ecological issues, there can be little disagreement that these finite resources need to be used with greater efficiency and care. The designers considered in this section have reappropriated the conventional and given us both inventive and elegant contemporary uses of the traditional – an essential skill in today's cutting-edge architecture of the interior.

Facing page:
Protected from the damaging effects of the sun, alabaster promotes a gentle, ambient, glow. This creates an interior not only sensitive to the day-to-day needs of the church, but also, perhaps more importantly, symbolic in terms of the role of light in the Catholic Church.

Weinerchaise

Name:
Weinerchaise

Location:
N/A

Date:
2009

Designer:
Andy Martin

It could be thought that a brick is a brick and that the opportunities for innovative use might be limited. The designer Andy Martin has reinterpreted the use of the brick to create a product that, in image at least, is seen as being essential to interior space: the chair.

Certainly the *Weinerchaise* is a striking form that reconsiders one of the most basic of building materials – it is not reported how comfortable it is to sit on.

Above:
Extruded, wire-cut, bricks are resin-bonded accurately in a mould before being carved by hand into the designed shape.

Cathedral of Our Lady of the Angels

Name:
Cathedral of Our Lady
of the Angels

Location:
Los Angeles, USA

Date:
2002

Designer:
Rafael Moneo

As we have seen in the previous section, both economic and environmental factors have had an impact on the use of mass materials in the design of spaces. At the same time, technology has enabled these same materials to be used in the interior with much greater creativity than ever before. Many contemporary designers have begun to appreciate again the qualities present in stone, brick and concrete.

Thinking such as this has enabled these materials to outlive changing fashions and to be used to produce innovative and creative projects that may well present us with the sense of permanence that has characterized materials of mass through the ages.

In the Cathedral of Our Lady of the Angels in Los Angeles the Spanish architect Rafael Moneo has used thin sheets of alabaster, a highly-figured stone, to allow natural light to penetrate the massive concrete walls of the cathedral.

Sustainability > **Innovations and the future**

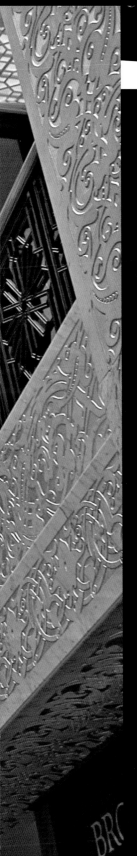

Metals

In our contemporary world it is difficult to imagine that there was a time when metals were not used in the construction of buildings and spaces. Steel and glass seem to be all around us and, for many, form the real fabric of our lives. The use of metal to create architectural forms has been inextricably linked to developments in technology over time and, in turn, the demands of society that come from those developments. What started as the ornamental use of elemental metals for their durability and beauty has developed to a point where much of the built environment could not exist without the opportunities that metals offer to build higher and wider and lighter than ever before.

Name:
Rookery Building
Location:
Chicago, USA
Date:
1888
Designer:
Daniel H Burnham and
John Wellborn Root

The wrought iron detailing of the interior of the Rookery Building has come to be a well-known example of art deco grillwork.

Metals have been used by man for many thousands of years, but for most of that time their use has been limited to what we think of as 'precious' metals: gold and silver and their poorer cousins bronze and brass. Renowned for their relative ease of extraction, malleability, durability and, probably above all, beauty, these elements and alloys have been at the forefront of the use of metals for much of human history. Due to their inherent qualities, they have been held as a representation of real and implied wealth – and still are – being largely used as coinage, jewellery and ornamentation in works of art and architecture. Places of worship, government, power and wealth – those places that society, or individuals, have deemed to be of the highest importance – have often attracted embellishment and decoration of surfaces and fittings with metals held in high esteem for their brilliance and lustre.

Facing page:
Bradbury Building,
Los Angeles, USA, 1893
The use of cast iron in this atrium is an example of technologies working together to allow for the first skyscrapers.

The Industrial Revolution

There are records of iron being cast into weapons and ornamentation from the sixth century and cannons cast from iron were still being produced until the late eighteenth century, but the use of iron in construction did not start to become commonplace until the late 1770s when engineers such as Darby, Paine and Telford used iron beams in the construction of bridges. Within buildings, the ability to replace stone, timber beams and columns with cast iron enabled the construction of wide, open spaces, better suited to the new demands of industrial production. For the designers and engineers of the time, it was clearly difficult to separate the qualities and opportunities of stone and timber with those of the new material.

Throughout the industrial era, decoration was cast into iron in the same way that it had traditionally been applied to stone and timber.

The process of casting iron using early techniques of mass production meant that structural elements were able to be manufactured in large numbers to a consistent design and quality. This ability to mass-produce buildings and spaces on an industrial scale, hastened and drove the Industrial Revolution. An icon of this time, the Crystal Palace in London, UK, was an iron and steel hall conceived and designed by Joseph Paxton to house the Great Exhibition of 1851. It contained an area of almost 92,000 m^2 and took just 17 weeks to build.

Victorian

Industrial production and expansion were key to the economic and social success of the Victorian era. The ability to rapidly reproduce accurate building elements (columns and beams) led to ever larger spaces being constructed to house the machinery and workforce needed to process and manufacture goods from across the empire.

The opportunity to sell these goods to an increasing middle class also demanded that the new materials and construction techniques be employed in designing spaces that had never before existed in society. Shopping, as an activity, began to appear in the late eighteenth and early nineteenth centuries. Shops and shoppers were grouped and contained in some of the most elaborate examples of Victorian iron and glass architecture. Natural light flooded in through glass rooves, allowing social interaction and trade to take place whatever the weather.

Having installed his first passenger elevator in 1857, Elisha Otis took buildings skywards. Iron, as the supporting frame for a building, allowed skyscrapers to develop and Mr Otis' invention allowed people to live and work at heights, and at a density, never before imagined.

Metals

The aesthetic movements

With iron and steel firmly established
as the primary structural materials
for the majority of commercial and industrial
buildings from the mid-nineteenth century,
the application of metals in the interior as
decoration also began to be considered.
In contrast to the historical obsession
with silver and gold as a representation
of importance and wealth, the working and
application of metal became prominent
as a demonstration of the skill, craft and
honesty of the metalworker – as befitted the
philosophy of the design movements of the
time. With the steel structure of buildings
becoming increasingly rational, interiors
were where the essential qualities of metals
were best exhibited.

Above:
The Bon Marché/Macy's,
Seattle, USA, 1890
Bronze grillwork such as this
is widely used in buildings
from the late-nineteenth and
early twentieth centuries.

Facing page:
Kirche am Steinhof, Vienna,
Austria, Otto Wagner, 1907
The altar and the baldachin
exemplify the Viennese
Secessionist use of gilded
copper.

No longer limited to spaces of power, the
craftsman was able to capitalize on the
many qualities inherent in these basic
materials: the play of light on a glided figure;
the rough coldness of wrought iron; the
satisfying ring of metal closing against
metal – details that stimulated the senses
and held a memory of their physical
processes of creation.

History and context > International icons

Left:
Ring Cafe, Dresden,
Germany, c.1960
Many modernist structures
such as this were characterized
by a combination of steel,
concrete and glass.

Facing page:
Steel Bar and Grill,
Sydney, Australia,
Dreamtime, 1999
Restaurant bathrooms
entirely in stainless steel
fittings and finishes.

Modernism

The combination of steel, concrete and glass characterized much of the form of the modernist period. Slender steel structures were often used to separate the concrete ground and ceiling planes, with large expanses of glass completing the voids in between.

The use of metals in the interior reflected the rationality and functionality of the architecture: clean lines and pure forms were used for architectural elements such as balustrades and doors. In a continuation of the aspirations of aestheticism, but eschewing the need for ornamentation and decoration, modernist designers made full use of the attention to detail provided by the craftsman and the quality of form provided by the material.

Postmodern and contemporary

Due to advances in alloy technologies and methods of manufacture, metals have re-emerged as a material that can be deployed in the interior. Traditionally seen as culturally ambiguous, often hard, cold and unfriendly and not a natural choice for the interior, metals today are abundantly found as coverings and claddings.

Historically connected with wealth and importance, the use of gold and silver are now often perceived as being 'in poor taste'. Contemporary design instead makes extensive use of stainless steel, chrome and anodized aluminium in a variety of finishes. Craftsmanship and the inherent qualities of metal – the ability to take on forms, to bend, to be wrought, to be textured and patinated – have been given over to a machine aesthetic that presents metals as the sterile product of a mechanical process, largely removed from the marks of the individual.

Metals

'What is the chief characteristic of the tall office building? It is lofty. It must be tall. The force and power of altitude must be in it, the glory and pride of exaltation must be in it. It must be every inch a proud and soaring thing, rising in sheer exaltation that from bottom to top it is a unit without a single dissenting line.'

Louis Sullivan

Metals are ubiquitous in the construction of buildings around us. They provide the structural backbone to much of our built environment, but in doing so are often hidden beneath layers of covering and cladding. The interiors shown in this section concentrate on the qualities that metals bring to a space: texture, patination, strength and ductility. The opportunity to take on texture and ornamentation, the application of surface finishes, the ability to be bent, twisted, hammered, rolled and wrought – the inherent nature of metal – are all exemplified here.

Robert Atkinson

Name:
The Daily Express Building

Location:
London, UK

Date:
1932 (restored 2002 by
John Robertson Architects)

Designer:
Robert Atkinson

Originally designed by Sir Evan Owen Williams (1890–1969), the home of the *Daily Express* newspaper was one of the finest examples of art deco design in London. With an exterior of black glass, Vitrolite panels, chromium strips at the joints and chamfered corner windows, the building presented the best of streamlined design as the expression of a modern and progressive newspaper. The interior could not have been more contrasting. Influenced by his love of cinema and the glamour of Hollywood, the Scottish architect Robert Atkinson (1883–1953) created a starburst ceiling in gold- and silver-leaf laid over plaster reliefs by Eric Aumonier depicting aspects of industry.

When combined with walls of travertine, black marble, bright metal fittings, a floor pattern of blue and black rubber outlined by narrow green strips and subtle lighting, the effect is to dazzle the visitor with the dynamism of the newspaper and the exuberance of the age.

'The longer I work in this building the more
I notice about it, the leaves unfurling on the pillars
upstairs in the upstairs gallery, the forestry feel
when you look across the museum from upstairs.
It sometimes feels like it's alive and growing when
you're not looking.'

Flora Bain

Deane & Woodward

Name:
The Oxford University
Museum

Location:
Oxford, UK

Date:
1860

Designer:
Deane & Woodward

Winning favour with the university authorities over a classical design by Barry, this neo-Gothic museum was heavily influenced by the ideas of John Ruskin in its use of materials and decoration. Designed to bring as much light into the building as possible, and making use of the production techniques of the time, the iron and glass structure originally proved too heavy and was redesigned by E A Skidmore. The resulting structure exemplifies the opportunities that the use of cast iron brought to the new museums: light, open interiors able to accommodate both the large collections that had been amassed by Victorian explorers as well as the large number of visitors that came to see them.

The opportunities that iron gave to apply decoration and fine detail were also used to allow the structure of the building to act as an expression of the purpose and aspiration of the museum. Wrought ironwork in the spandrels and at the tops of the columns represented branches of various species of tree, including sycamore, walnut and palm.

Facing page :
The entrance hall by Atkinson
(restored lobby by John
Robertson Architects in 2002).

Above:
A Victorian-Gothic revival
combination of structure and
ornamentation that echoes
the surroundings and context.

History and context > International icons > Sustainability

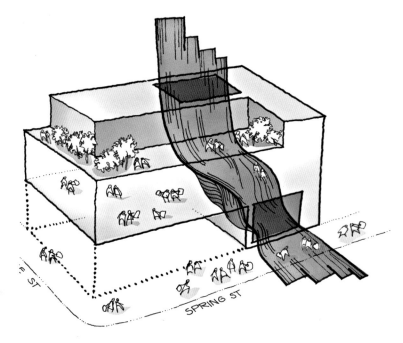

Heatherwick Studio

Name:
La Maison Unique
for Longchamp

Location:
New York, USA

Date:
2006

Designer:
Heatherwick Studio

Undertaking the extensive remodelling of an existing SoHo building, Heatherwick studio used the installation of a 'landscape staircase' as an opportunity to cut a three-storey void through the structure, bringing natural light into the store and opening up a very small street frontage. Using steel also allowed for magnetic product display and lighting to be attached and moved around the staircase, ensuring that the installation was very much part of the sales experience and not simply a means to access each floor. The staircase acts as an element 'bringing daylight down and people up'; the form of the steel and the glass balustrade are undoubtedly reminiscent of the fall and folds of the fabrics and fashion that the client is famous for.

Above:
Studio sketches show how the staircase acts as an inserted element, bringing people from the street through the store and out to the roof garden.

Facing page:
The staircase is constructed from 55 tonnes of hot-rolled steel.

'…an installation that divides and converges to form a topography of walkways, landings and steps.'

Heatherwick Studio

The efficient design and use of metals, which are a finite resource, is key to the long-term sustainability of the material. Contemporary software and computing power enable engineers and designers, often adopting the 'cradle to cradle' principle, to create innovative and highly efficient structures that not only use the minimum of material but also span great distances allowing for the open and flexible use of interior space.

This efficient use of metals combined with the opportunity to recycle them when they reach the end of their useful life is being exploited by designers worldwide. The aesthetic qualities of specific metals, such as stainless steel with its flexibility, variety of finish and ease of reuse, is leading to elegant and beautiful interior designs that also aim to address environmental awareness.

Korban/Flaubert specialize in the use of recycled stainless steel. They maintain that the use of stainless steel (specifically, its long lifespan, 100 per cent recyclability and resistance to corrosion) allows it to outlast similar materials as well as doing away with the need for expensive and often chemically harmful finishes and coatings.

Project Import Export of Miami is a multi-disciplinary studio committed to the use of renewable and sustainable natural resources as well as the use of non-toxic additives in the processing of those resources. Their stainless steel and aluminium furniture uses all recycled strips, adhering to the cradle-to-cradle ethic.

In the mass market the production of interior elements such as floor, wall, bathroom and kitchen modules all lend themselves well to the use of a variety of metals, such as lightweight steel and aluminium. Many contemporary steel-framed buildings are built with their potential future dismantling as a key design feature; equally many are constructed with the possibility of extension and addition built in.

The construction industry, engineers, architects and interior architects need to continue the drive for greater efficiency in the design, manufacture and use of metals in order to bring costs and energy use down and again open up the opportunity to make greater use of one of the most potentially diverse materials.

Metals

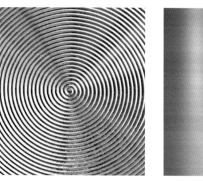

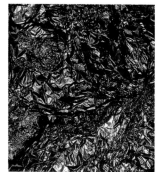

It could be argued that with the widespread use of steel as one of the main structural systems in architecture, the use of metals in interior architecture has come full circle. The ability to be worked into a variety of forms, to have textures and finishes applied and to be responsive to the visual and acoustic qualities of a space, has resulted in the re-appropriation of metals as an important and expressive interior material. The example here demonstrates how those inherent qualities discussed have been used in an unexpected but ingenious context.

Below:
Main auditorium stage curtain in collaboration with Pae White.

Metals

'Metafoil takes advantage of the captive gaze of the audience, introducing a foil, a false reflection, an illusion of depth, a novel typography that disrupts expectation and challenges perception.'

Pae White

Metafoil curtain at the Royal Norwegian Opera

Name:
Metafoil curtain at the Royal Norwegian Opera

Location:
Oslo, Norway

Date:
2008

Designer:
Snøhetta Architects with Pae White

Clearly defined concepts at the earliest stage of this design ensured that the opera house would meet the requirements of the client. Three 'diagrams' were driven through to the completed design: the 'wave wall'; the 'factory' and the 'carpet'.

The architects saw the 'factory', or production facilities of the opera house as a distinct element within the design, deserving of rational planning and use of materials. Aluminium cladding was used throughout these areas.

The stage curtain in the main auditorium was seen as a key 'threshold' where the aims (and contrasting design treatment) of the 'factory' met the needs of the public. Collaboration with American artist Pae White, who has worked with woven textiles, light and optical effects, resulted in digital images of aluminium foil being studied for their reflection and adoption of the lights and colours of the auditorium. These images were then transferred to a computer-controlled loom that wove the curtain. The artist, and her 'Metafoil' has succeeded in achieving a dramatic, three-dimensional, sculptural effect on a two-dimensional surface.

In 1753 Marc-Antoine Laugier published his
Essai sur l'Architecture in which he suggested
that the 'primitive hut' was humanity's
fundamental architectural response to the
basic need of shelter. Whether this is considered
to be the first theory of architecture or not,
wood has always been regarded as the most
basic of building materials. Using tools that
have changed little over thousands of years,
humanity has succeeded in felling, converting
and fashioning timber into architectural
and artistic forms that owe their diversity,
function and beauty as much to the location,
species and qualities of the woods used as
they do to the skills of those who worked them.

Like the use of stone discussed in Chapter One, wood is a natural resource that can be shaped and worked to provide not only the structural requirements of a shelter but also the artistic and functional finishes of the interior. In contrast to stone, wood rots. Whilst we have timber buildings and structures that have lasted for many hundreds of years (often depending on the climatic and environmental conditions in which they exist), structures from ancient times have long since disappeared. Due to its lack of permanence, wood was often used for structures of lesser importance, with stone being reserved for those buildings that were intended to last. A notable exception to this were the Buddhist temples of Japan, some of which are thought to be amongst the oldest wooden structures in the world, dating back over 1,000 years.

Again, in contrast to stone, timber can be easily cut into manageable sizes that allow for a shelter to be built by just a few people or by an individual. Indigenous peoples, such as the Navajo of North America, have used wooden poles, often made weathertight with bark and mud, to construct simple but effective homes.

Right:
Interior of a Navajo house or 'hogan'
A conical interior of stacked wooden poles; covered on the outside with bark and mud to provide protection against the weather. The entrance to the hogan would face east so that the interior would get the morning sun as well as a daily blessing for the family.

Early history

The problems of rot, fungal and insect attack have never detracted from the ease of use of timber in construction. It is easy to forget that many of the impressive stone ruins that remain from ancient times often had roofs, internal walls, doors and fittings of elaborately carved wood, making them habitable spaces. Where these buildings of importance have been maintained, we are still able to see where the structural qualities and aesthetic brilliance of wood has been used to convey the most powerful messages and most dramatic interiors. The soaring spaces of many of the medieval churches and cathedrals of Europe were only possible thanks to the skill of the carpenter in providing the supporting frameworks, whilst many tonnes of stone were assembled around them. The benches and pews, stalls, altars, choirs, screens, fonts and, most dramatically, roofs display a level of skill and artistry that not only create the functional interior but also provide the narrative so important in Christian places of worship.

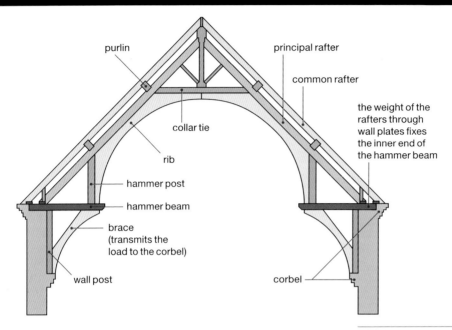

purlin

principal rafter

common rafter

collar tie

the weight of the rafters through wall plates fixes the inner end of the hammer beam

rib

hammer post

hammer beam

brace
(transmits the load to the corbel)

wall post

corbel

The relative cheapness of timber construction also meant that the vast majority of everyday buildings used timber for their structure. Interestingly, the expression of this timber structure was clear both inside and out, rather than being hidden (as was often the case with more expensive, prestigious buildings in stone and brick).

Advances in the understanding of the distribution of the weight of heavy church roofs led carpenters to construct 'hammer-beam' roofs where, in a similar idea to stone vaulting, the timber roof is able to span a larger space than the use of single, tie beams would normally allow.

As developments were made in the understanding of structures and the use of timber, construction methods and the tools used remained largely unchanged for hundreds of years.

Above:
Simple diagram of a hammer-beam roof
This diagram shows the primary elements and principles of load distribution in a hammer-beam roof.

Facing page:
Tithe barn, Bradford-on-Avon, UK, early fourteenth century
Timber roofs such as this were a cheaper and easier option than the stone constructions that had gone before them.

Discussion point:
Structure in the middle ages

In many buildings from this period, the wooden structure was, unusually, left visible (previously, the structure of buildings had been hidden).

● How visible are the structural materials used in modern architecture?

● Which materials now tend to be used for structural purposes?

The Renaissance, Georgian and Regency

Like many of the interiors and architecture explored in this book already, artistry and craft, whether it be in stone or wood, was reserved for the most important of buildings: those of rulers and of the church. The wealthy merchants and nobility of the Renaissance looked to adorn their homes with luxurious finishes. The variety, uniqueness and subtle beauty of wood provided an accessible resource with which to embellish the home and the exuberance of Renaissance Italy provided the opportunity.

Marquetry and parquetry flourished in sixteenth-century Florence and Naples. In both techniques, thin veneers of exotic woods (as well as semi-precious stones such as onyx, jasper and lapis lazuli) were applied to wooden objects, furniture and panelling to create images and patterns – parquetry usually refers to geometric designs whereas marquetry often refers to the creation of decorative designs or pictures. Through the use of fine cutting techniques, sanding, staining, and the balancing and mirroring of wood grain, texture and colour, incredibly intricate and visually complex designs were created. Like so much to do with the use of wood, many of these techniques have remained unchanged and are still in use today.

As a result of the Industrial Revolution, and with the development of large-scale cast iron frames still some years off, the decorative excesses of Georgian Europe were put to one side as the need to construct spaces to aid the expansion in trade and industrial and imperial power became paramount. Owing to the technological achievements of the medieval craftsmen who had come before, wooden construction at this time was pushed to its limits to create some of the most dramatic and beautiful spaces that we still have with us today.

'I don't like things that can be reproduced. Wood isn't important in itself but rather in the fact that objects made in it are unique, simple, unpretentious.'

Georg Baselitz

Above:
Number 3 Slip,
Chatham Dockyard, Kent,
UK, 1838
A massive timber frame of square-section timber aisle posts with iron bases and knees.

Right:
Interior of Collingham
Gardens, London, UK,
by Ernest George and
Peto Architects, 1880s
Late-Victorian panelling in
a revivalist Queen Anne style.

Victorian and the aesthetic movements

With the development of cast iron and steel for the structural frames of many of the important buildings of the late nineteenth century, wood reverted to being used for interior partitions, fittings and decoration (although timber was, and is, still used for basic construction on a more domestic scale).

True to the Victorian penchant for revivalist styles, medieval and Gothic roofs, screens and carving were all abundant in the religious, civic and domestic interiors of the time.

Wooden panelling was popular in the homes of the wealthy Victorian middle classes, reminiscent of the great, stately houses with their panelled galleries; this fashion lasted in the suburbs of England right through to the 1930s.

Modernism

In its reaction to the revivalists of the Victorian era, the Arts and Crafts movement looked to promote a new honesty with a return to the traditional carving of wood as objects and for interiors. But at the start of the twentieth century, the use of timber was moving along with the modernist ideal of the machine age and new materials were on display and their opportunities were being exploited.

To make more economic use of expensive wooden finishes, engineered woods were developed. The most familiar of these is plywood, where thin layers of wood are laminated together with glue to produce a material that is extremely strong, resistant to moisture and insect attack and, most importantly, does not suffer from the twisting and warping associated with natural timbers. When given a highly figured or hardwood finish as the top layer, plywood construction can give the appearance of being far more expensive and exotic than it really is. Combined with the opportunities it creates for forming curves and three-dimensional shapes, its use was highlighted by many modernist designers as both an interior finish and in furniture construction.

Below:
Venesta Display Stand, Building Exhibition, London, UK, by Skinner and Tecton, 1934
This stand was designed to show off the applicability of plywood to construction. Under the direction of Jack Pritchard, Venesta had become one of the most enlightened architectural patrons of the period.

History and context > International icons

Contemporary use

It may sound obvious but wood is a product of trees, and some trees can take many, many years to grow to maturity before their wood can be used. Native hardwoods, such as oak and walnut and their tropical cousins, teak and mahogany, have figured prominently in much of the design that we have looked at in this chapter. Their extensive use was possible due to large areas of the world supporting ancient forests that had remained untouched for generations. Many of these forests, resulting from indiscriminate logging and poor management, have no more wood to give and it will be many more generations before some of these species will grow again. Wood, like so many natural materials, has become an expensive and valuable commodity that has to be used sparingly, or has to be replaced by similar, but inferior artificial materials.

In contemporary design and interiors, wood is again being appreciated for its quality and beauty, but consideration has to be given to its responsible use. Designers such as Ando, Arad, de Feo, Fujimoto, Snøhetta and Zumthor all succeed in giving a sense of craft to their use of timber. Their demonstration of the use and potential of fine woods in a contemporary context take us back to a time when the craftsman understood his material and how to get the best from it.

Above:
The Norwegian National Opera and Ballet, Oslo, Norway, by Snøhetta Architects, 2008
As one of the 'visible' elements of architecture (the others being stone, metal (aluminium) and glass) wooden panels (oak) were used to emphasize the 'carpet' that would tie the different areas and conditions of the building together.

'My art is an attempt to reach beyond the surface appearance. I want to see growth in wood, time in stone, nature in a city, and I do not mean its parks but a deeper understanding that a city is nature too – the ground upon which it is built, the stone with which it is made.'

Andy Goldsworthy

Discussion point:
Alternatives to wood

Spend some time looking around the spaces that you use at home and work.

- How many objects and surfaces are made of wood? How many of these are in fact made of engineered wood (such as plywood and chipboard) or laminates applied to non-wood bases (such as cardboard) or, in fact, fake wood (such as photographic representations of wood)?

- Why do you think these have not been made from 'real' wood?

- How would the feel, smell, texture, appearance and quality of these items be different if they had been made from 'real' wood?

The appeal of wood and the understanding of its qualities by those who work with it have not diminished. It is warm to the touch, can be smooth, rough or textured; the natural grain of wood reveals unique and ever-changing patterns that can be emphasized by careful machining or the application of surface treatments; some woods are naturally resistant to fire, moisture, chemical and insect attack, others change and move as they are exposed to the environment; some can take intricate and precise detail at the hands of the craftsman and all will always result in the creation of something beautiful and unique.

The two projects considered here, one of them well known, one not so well known, have been designed by people who clearly understand and appreciate the material that they are working with. They exemplify the use of timber in its most basic converted form and assembled in a way that emphasizes that form. The resulting structures present us with environments where the feel, texture, colour, smell and sound of wood are given precedence over everything else.

Facing page:
Interior
Timber beams are stacked and braced by steel structures.

Peter Zumthor

Name:
The Swiss Pavilion, 'Sound Box'
Location:
Expo 2000, Hanover
Date:
2000
Designer:
Peter Zumthor

The son of a furniture maker and master joiner, it is perhaps not surprising that Zumthor is renowned for his respect and love of materials. Each of his spaces and buildings give a sense of being handcrafted and intimately connected with the location in which they sit, the techniques from which they are constructed and the materials from which they are made.

This temporary pavilion was designed to give a flavour of Switzerland and was intended by Zumthor to create a *Gesamtkunstwerk* – a term used by the composer Richard Wagner to define an ideal combination of performing arts, music, drama and decor into a form of total theatre.

It is clear from what Zumthor has said that the space itself should be as simple as possible, to provide a backdrop against which his 'total theatre' should take place. The wood used was larch and Douglas pine from the forests of Switzerland (sustainably and responsibly harvested) and it is not hard to imagine that, once in this space, the smell, feel and sounds of the country from which the wood had come would be all around – the experience of Switzerland would indeed be total.

'Taking the Expo theme of sustainability seriously, we constructed the pavilion out of 144 km of lumber with a cross-section of 20 x 10 cm, totalling 2,800 cubic metres of larch and Douglas pine from Swiss forests, assembled without glue, bolts or nails, only braced with steel cables, and with each beam being pressed down on the one below. After the closure of the Expo, the building was dismantled and the beams sold as seasoned timber.'

Peter Zumthor

Right:
Every element of the house
is as important as every other.

Sou Fujimoto Architects

Name:
Final Wooden House

Location:
Kumamoto, Japan

Date:
2008

Designer:
Sou Fujimoto Architects

'Lumber is extremely versatile.
In an ordinary wooden
architecture, lumber is effectively
differentiated according to
functions in various localities
precisely because it is so
versatile. Columns, beams,
foundations, exterior walls,
interior walls, ceilings, floorings,
insulations, furnishings, stairs,
window frames, meaning all.
However, I thought if lumber
is indeed so versatile then
why not create architecture by
one rule that fulfils all of these
functions. I envisioned the
creation of new spatiality that
preserves primitive conditions
of a harmonious entity before
various functions and roles
differentiated.'
Sou Fujimoto

Japan has a proud history of
timber construction, with several
of its Buddhist temples being
some of the oldest wooden
buildings in the world. In this
innovative exercise in building
with wood, Sou Fujimoto
has made a contemporary
connection with his heritage.
By dissolving the traditional
boundaries and functions
between the building elements:
column, beam, wall, interior
and exterior, he has succeeded
in creating an environment
where every piece of timber
used is not only integral to the
success of the structure but
also provides a space and a
place for something to happen.

In a similar vein to the Zumthor
pavilion (see pp062+063),
large raw sections of local
timber have been stacked and
mechanically fixed. The simplicity
of the construction technique
belie the complexity of the
design process in conceiving
of a three-dimensional house
where every 'wall' and 'floor'
element become surfaces on
and in which to inhabit the space.

As Sou Fujimoto explains,
'there are no separations of floor,
wall, and ceiling here. A place
that one thought was a floor
becomes a chair, a ceiling,
a wall from various positions.
The floor levels are relative and
spatiality is perceived differently
according to one's position.
Here, people are distributed
three-dimensionally in the space.
This is a place like an amorphous
landscape with a new experience
of various senses of distances.
Inhabitants discover, rather
than being prescribed, various
functionalities in these
convolutions.'

Built in a woodland setting,
the house provides the occupant
with the Japanese equivalent
of the *Gesamtkunstwerk*
(referenced by Zumthor in the
Sound Box): the total physical
and sensory experience
of Japan.

Below:
Stacked sections of timber provide structure, to create places of rest and activity.

'This bungalow no longer fits the category of wooden architecture. If wooden architecture is merely something made from wood, then wood itself surpasses the architectural procedures to directly become a 'place where people live' in this bungalow. It is of an existence akin to primitive conditions before architecture. Rather than just a new architecture, this is a new origin, a new existence.'

Sou Fujimoto

The historical and contemporary designs illustrated in this chapter have shown how wood can be used to create the most beautiful environments and the most unique designs. Many of these have been on a relatively small scale and have made use of timbers from around the world that are often, today, unavailable. Technological developments in the use of veneers and engineered woods have allowed progressive and skilled designers to create interiors and furniture that have not relied on the use of large quantities of exotic species – however the processes involved in the manufacture of these new materials are themselves often called into question.

According to the Forest Stewardship Council (an international, non-governmental organization dedicated to promoting responsible management of the world's forests) much of the timber imported into the UK and the US is the product of illegal and irresponsible logging across many of the world's forests.

Once the forests are gone they are lost forever and the resulting damage to the global ecological balance could be unstoppable. The FSC manages over 75 forests worldwide and aims for products used in the construction industry to be traceable back to their location of origin; thereby assuring the supplier and the consumer of ethical and sustainable sourcing. Greenpeace reports that in 2006 the UK consumed 1.34 million cubic metres of plywood with 750,000 cubic metres of this being from unsustainable, tropical sources.

In 2008, the Gaudi European Student Competition on Sustainable Architecture was won by two students from the University of Vienna, Andreas Claus Schnetzer and Pils Gregor, with their design for a sustainable, recyclable shelter constructed out of timber pallets. The design, called 'Pallet-Haus', provides modular, energy-efficient (power and water is routed through the spaces between the pallet layers) and affordable housing that requires the minimal use of additional materials.

Whilst making use of a commercial timber product, the pallet, the resulting structure not only demonstrates a clear understanding of the use and potential of a basic, recyclable wooden element but also succeeds in creating a rhythmic and beautiful space that can help and be functional in a variety of situations and environments.

International icons > **Sustainability** > Innovations and the future

The future use of timber in design and construction would seem to centre around many of the issues illustrated in the previous section. Being, in many cases, a finite resource, the responsible choice, specification and harvesting of timber is key to its long-term availability. Whilst the traditional use of tropical hardwoods has decreased, we now find that many of these same species are being used for engineered wood products such as plywood. Given the environmental damage that foresting these species causes, it seems inexcusable that a material once used to make the finest carvings, furniture and interiors should end up being used in the production of something so banal as plywood.

Smaller scale, beautiful, contemporary work is, thankfully, still being done. Salvaged and recycled soft and hardwoods provide the raw material for some of the finest designers and craftsmen today to produce unique items.

Vortex Credenza sideboard

Name:
'Vortex Credenza'

Location:
N/A

Date:
2008

Designer:
David Linley

This piece plays with geometry. Although it is in fact the traditional rectangular shape of a sideboard, the overall look is distorted by op art rosewood and sycamore marquetry veneering. The drawers are lined in surprising textures and make use of vibrant colours and materials, such as gold leaf and padded velvet, thus adding to the overall sensual experience.

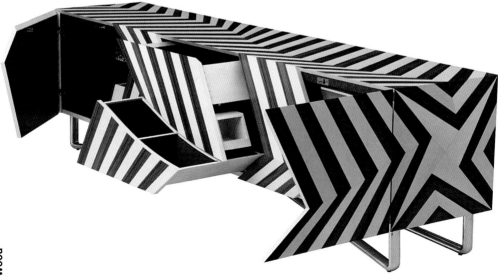

Community chest of drawers

Name:
Community

Location:
N/A

Date:
2009

Designer:
Rob Southcott

Rob Southcott's 'Community' chest of drawers, made from a 'select variety of locally reclaimed timber species' reflects the 'growing diversity found in contemporary society' and is meant to symbolize a 'vision of multiculturalism'.

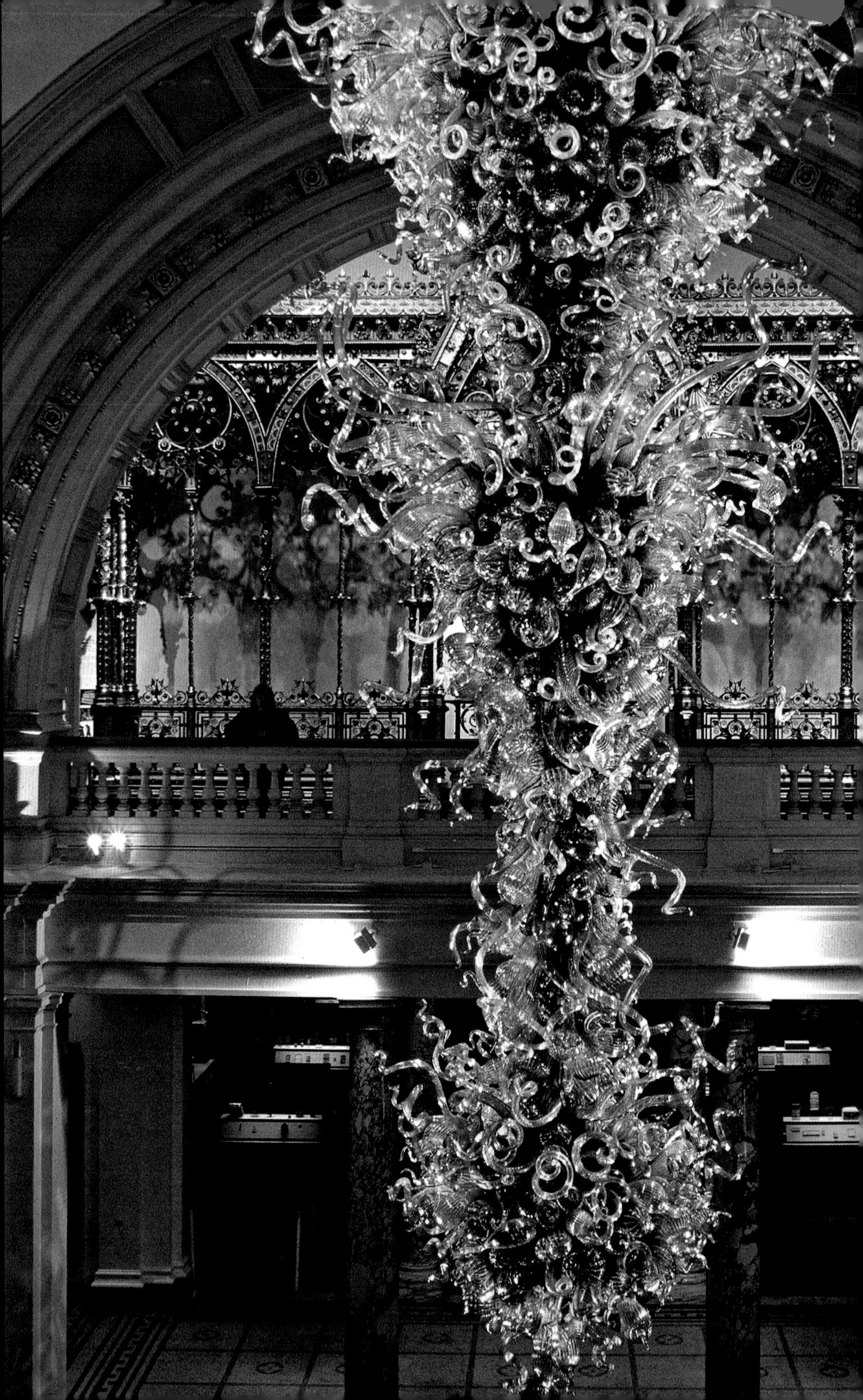

Glass occupies a very special place in the design
of buildings and spaces. It could be said that
we use it to fill the gaps in our buildings. In doing
so, we illuminate the world in which we live, work
and play. Throughout history, glass has been used
to allow light into the spaces that we create but
the illumination of our lives has come to mean
something far more profound than just the ability
to see. Glass can be a simple window but this
combination of sand, soda and lime has long been
used, especially in a religious context, to transmit
the knowledge and imagery of faith. Glass can
be decorative and can be a surface on which
to apply decoration. Glass can emphasize space,
material and structure and allow us to see
aspects of construction that have never been
seen before. Glass, and the ability to create
more void than solid, has been the primary
driver behind architectural design for the past
150 years. And now, finally, glass has become
a material in its own right, creating, supporting
and, of course, illuminating, our lives.

Name:
Chandelier at the
Victoria & Albert Museum

Location:
London, UK

Date:
2001

Designer:
Dale Chihuly

Each element of the chandelier
was individually crafted and then
assembled on site.

Archaeological evidence of the use of glass as vessels and beads has been found to date as far back as 3000 BC. The production of glass for use in an architectural context was not common until the Romans used it from around AD 100. However, to say that it was in common usage would be an exaggeration: glass was a luxury material and was only used in the most important of buildings. It took another thousand years, and developments in the manufacturing processes (using easily available potash from wood ashes), before glass would be seen regularly in important religious and secular buildings.

Early medieval Christian glass

By the eleventh century it had been discovered that the addition of impurities to the glass-making process would colour the material. Stained glass, which was in general use from the twelfth century, is usually thought of in relation to the great cathedrals and churches of Europe. Moving on from the heavier Romanesque style, religious buildings took on the more vertical, Gothic look that came to dominate through to the early Renaissance. As has been noted in Chapter One, the skill of the mason led to the structure, the solid parts of the building, being reduced to a minimum. Cathedrals went higher and wider with innovations such as the pointed arch allowing vast, open spaces to be created.

Height and verticality were seen as being synonymous with moving towards the heavens and the increased amount of void between the stone allowed for light to flood in. What could be better, then, than to fill these spaces with the most richly coloured glass? Especially when it could be used to depict religious imagery and stories to a largely illiterate population.

Facing page:
Rose window, Notre Dame, Paris, France, 1250
An example of an early medieval, Christian, stained-glass window.

The use of coloured glass to depict religious imagery was, in the main, restricted to the Christian world. In Islam, figurative representations of humans and animals are largely rejected; religious buildings are often decorated in calligraphy depicting passages and quotations from the Qur'an instead. Clear and coloured glass were, of course, used to great effect bringing light to places of worship but its symbolic use was of less importance to that of illuminating the dramatically decorated interiors of mosques and temples.

Above:
Hagia Sophia, Istanbul, Turkey, AD 532–537
The use of many windows at the base of the main dome not only highlights the elaborate decoration but gives the impression of the dome floating, increasing the sense of the vastness of space.

Industrial Revolution and the Victorian era

The use of glass and stained glass for symbolic reasons remained the norm in religious buildings in Europe and North America right through to the nineteenth and twentieth centuries. The use of glass to fill the voids of a structural skeleton can, as we have seen, trace its roots back to the Gothic architecture of the medieval period. The revivalist fervour of the Victorian era, combined with the industrial developments that brought the mass production of cast iron structures, allowed the use of glass to be taken to new heights – literally.

Above:
Palm House,
Royal Botanic Gardens, Kew,
UK, Decimus Burton, 1848
The Victorian fascination with plant species from around the world and the need to maintain the habitats from which they had originated were a perfect opportunity to marry contemporary industrial techniques with elegant Victorian design.

The Victorians travelled the world collecting plant specimens. To keep them healthy and to allow them to grow, engineers and designers came together to construct magnificent glasshouses, many of which can still be visited today. Gothic stone was replaced with cast iron (often equally heavily ornamented) allowing, for the first time, the amount of glass to be greater than the structure supporting it.

History and context > International icons

Above:
Crown Bar Liquor Saloon,
Belfast, UK, 1885
Close-up of the highly ornate
restored interior of decorative
tiles, wooden fixtures and
etched glass panes.

The transparent opportunities of glass
delighted the Victorian builder and the
symbolic opportunities afforded by such
'transparency' were not lost either. In
an age of strict social conformity, glass
was used on a smaller scale to attempt
to control behaviour. Drinking was frowned
upon and elaborately decorated and
etched screens and windows were installed
in public houses to 'protect' polite society
from the drunken rabble.

Reform of a more serious nature, in the
form of prisons, or penitentiaries, connected
social correction with religion and this was
reflected in the spaces constructed to house
those who were in need of 'correction'.

When one looks at a contemporary version,
the same connection is easy to make.

The aesthetic movements

The artists and designers of the Arts and Crafts movement had no such hang-ups about the symbolic nature of glass. In their view, decoration was simply a positive application of materials and methods, if it exemplified the quality of craft and the craftsman. In a rejection of the confused stylistic language of the Victorians, designers such as Morris and Voysey turned instead to the opportunities that the interplay of light, glass and colour could bring to the uncomplicated interiors that they were building.

Above:
Chicago Cultural Center,
Chicago, USA, 1897
The Preston Bradley Hall
is dominated by the Tiffany
glass dome.

Perhaps the most renowned artist specializing in the decorative qualities of glass was Louis Comfort Tiffany. Inspired by the ideals of Morris and the Arts and Crafts movement, Tiffany trained as a fine artist. He soon developed an interest in glass and in the late 1800s began to make a name for himself as an interior designer producing, amongst many notable works, glass screens for the White House in 1882. The first Tiffany Glass Company was incorporated on 1 December, 1885, and in 1902 became known as the Tiffany Studios.

History and context > International icons

Modernism

What could better exemplify the
ideals of modernism than glass and
its combined use with steel and concrete?
The rationalization of structure, a process
that, as we have seen, had progressed
on and off for the past millennium, reached
its logical conclusion: slim concrete slabs
seemed to float with only the minimal use
of slender steel to support them. The barrier
between the interior of the space and the
landscape surrounding the buildings were
dissolved – save for a thin layer of glass.

The technological developments that
had taken architectural design to this point
were considerable but a logical progression.
Glass was inextricably linked to the
structural opportunities of steel and
steel-reinforced concrete – natural light
flooded in and illuminated interiors as
never before.

**Above:
Farnsworth House,
Illinois, USA, by
Ludwig Mies van der Rohe,
1951**
There is seemingly no 'wall'
between the interior and the
landscape.

'Find beauty not only in the thing itself but in the pattern of the shadows, the light and dark which that thing provides.'

Junichiro Tanizaki

Postmodern and contemporary

In 1933, writer Junichiro Tanizaki wrote an essay on aesthetics, called *In Praise of Shadows*. In the essay he examined the Western obsession with progress and its continual search for light and clarity – key modernist ideals made manifest in much of the architectural and interior design of today. Tanizaki argued at the time that in the East there was a greater understanding of light. There was, he argued, a greater appreciation of shadow and light in all its forms and that, historically, objects and interiors had been crafted to be seen in these constantly changing natural conditions.

Today, with the globalization of design, it could be argued that this has been lost: vast areas of glass and overwhelming light dominate our spaces. Many of us now permanently live and work as if on a stage set with the world as our uninvited audience.

Having said this, technology now enables us to use and appreciate the inherent qualities and structural opportunities that glass brings: it is now being used as a material in its own right and not just as a window.

History and context > International icons

We have seen that for millennia, craftsmen and designers have worked with the interaction of glass and light to produce some of the most dramatic and beautiful interior spaces. The two projects considered here exploit the partnership between light and glass to maximum effect, creating installations that bring everything together: lightness, delicacy, drama and spirituality – all that glass has given us over the past 5,000 years.

Facing page:
The final sculpture at its full 30 metre height.

Below:
The massed glass spheres.

Bottom:
Computer drawing showing the positioning of the sculpture in the space and an idea of the structural requirements necessary for its support.

Heatherwick Studio

Name:
Bleigiessen, The Wellcome Trust

Location:
London, UK

Date:
2005

Designer:
Heatherwick Studio

International biomedical research charity the Wellcome Trust, commissioned Heatherwick Studio to construct a sculpture for the atrium of their new headquarters. The eight-storey-high space rises above a pool and it was these two fundamental conditions, height and water, that gave inspiration to Heatherwick. The designer wanted to experiment with the dynamic shapes that are created when liquids fall. To do this he looked at *Bleigiessen* or 'lead guessing', a New Year activity in central Europe, where molten lead is dropped into water, producing shapes from which people predict their fortune for the coming year.

Over 400 of these experiments took place until a 5 cm-piece was selected that had the form the design team were looking for.

Having been digitized, the form was reproduced to span over thirty metres, by suspending 142,000 glass spheres on 27,000 high-tensile steel wires. Colour is constant and shifting by virtue of the dichroic film sandwiched within each glass sphere.

The ease with which Heatherwick speaks of the process behind the project belies the technical sophistication and structural complexities behind its success. As is often the case with interior architecture projects, the building and the space to be used were already in existence – the elements of the sculpture had to go through door openings already in place and be assembled on site.

The effect is no less stunning for Heatherwick's modesty in describing it. Driven by simple contextual factors and taking a lead from a natural, and cultural, physical process, materials, structure, technology and light have been brought together in a text-book design process that should inspire all students of interior architecture.

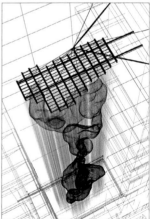

'The vertiginous quality of this space, coupled with the presence of water, suggested the idea of exploring ways of capturing the dynamic shapes of falling liquids.'

Thomas Heatherwick

FAM Arquitectos

Name:
Atocha Memorial

Location:
Madrid, Spain

Date:
2007

Designer:
FAM Arquitectos

As a lasting memorial to the victims of the Madrid bombings in 2004, FAM Arquitectos constructed an 11-metre-high glass tower that appears to rise out of the ground at Atocha Station, one of the sites of the blasts.

Visitors enter the memorial from an underground room accessed via the station. There they are able to look up into the tower and read thousands of messages of condolence left by members of the public immediately after the bombing.

The tower, constructed from 15,000 specially cast glass blocks held together with a transparent acrylic material that hardens as it is exposed to ultraviolet light, is lit only by the incidental light coming from the city. This background illumination allows visitors to look through the tower, to the sky, and read the messages printed onto an ETFE membrane, held in position on the inner wall of the tower. The sunlight hitting the tower is focused down to create a deep blue glow in the entrance chamber below. The chamber contains nothing except for a single steel bench where visitors can sit to contemplate the loss that is so graphically illustrated above them.

At night, the transparency and illuminating qualities of the glass allow the tower to glow from within.

The design and construction of this memorial demonstrates beautifully the enduring power of light, mediated by glass, to evoke emotion and atmosphere within spaces.

Below:
The blue room, a space to contemplate and remember.

Glass

Above:
The glass tower has a view to the sky, messages of condolence are inscribed on the inner wall and lit by the sun.

Left:
Visitors experience the message of the memorial from below.

Among all the materials considered in this book, glass is unique in that it can be infinitely recycled without compromising its quality or integrity. The manufacture of glass has long been a highly efficient process with minimal waste – although high energy consumption is undeniable.

Despite this, glass still makes up some 2.5 million tonnes of landfill in the UK and 9 billion litres in the US each year. Reclaimed or scrap glass, or 'cullet', can make up 80 per cent of the total mixture in jars and bottles; an average of 30 per cent of the make-up of the road material 'glasphalt' can be recycled glass and if glass is ground down to a small enough particle size it can be combined with cement to form a significantly strengthened concrete material. From the point of view of conventional, architectural use, products made from recycled glass have limitations in their consistency of colour and optical clarity. However, these variations have provided the opportunity for designers to experiment with innovative textures, finishes and colours.

The use of recycled and reclaimed glass techniques has had particular application in the design of interior spaces, with many contemporary materials being developed. Based on the traditional technique of terrazzo, where marble chips were bound together with a concrete mix, discarded glass is bound together in a similar way to produce counter tops and sanitary fittings that often use much less energy in their production as the glass does not have to be reformed. Waste glass is heated and fused to create objects and tiles that have unique patterns and textures – designers are using unwanted bottles and jars to create elegant and dynamic lighting installations. In short, the advantage that glass has in maintaining its quality throughout multiple recycling processes gives the designer the unique opportunity to create exciting and innovative objects and interior finishes.

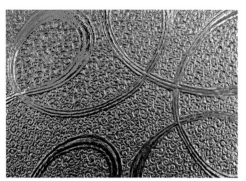

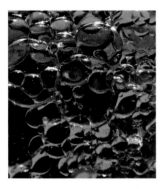

International icons > **Sustainability** > Innovations and the future

As noted previously, we are now in a time where, because of the technological developments in glass, we are able to use and appreciate this material for its own sake and not just as a transparent barrier to the weather. The combination of sand, lime and ash has come a long way from the simple containers of 5,000 years ago. Glass allows us to see into and illuminate our built environment; it contains our electrical production of light and, through fibre-optic cables, can transmit light as data over vast distances. What was once considered to be so fragile a material is now understood to be strong enough to support floors and roofs, much like steel. The seemingly endless possibilities of glass (it can be formed, toughened and decorated) has led many contemporary designers to use this material to create innovative design and not just to let light flood in.

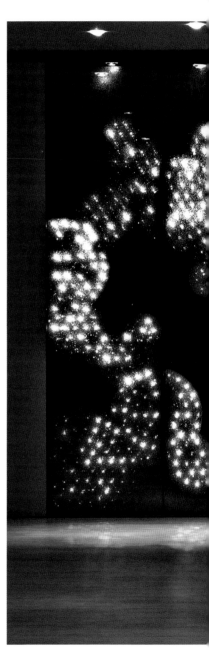

Honeycomb wall panel

Name:
Honeycomb wall panel

Location:
N/A

Date:
2009

Designer:
Swarovski

Swarovski have always worked with the essential quality of cut glass crystal – its ability to refract light. In this interior panel system, Swarovski have sandwiched thousands of tiny crystals into a tight, polycarbonate, honeycomb structure. Fibre-optic lighting – itself using glass technology – is fed in from behind and image and lighting effects play across the crystal screen. Limited only by the imagination of the client, these panels have been used to create entire shop windows that produce dazzling displays on a much larger scale than shown here.

Above:
Crystal screens are combined
with fibre-optic computer-
controlled lighting.

Sustainability > Innovations and the future

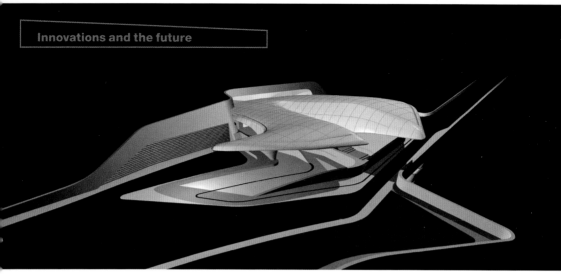

Hungerberg Railway Station

Name:
Hungerberg Railway Station

Location:
Innsbruck, Austria

Date:
2007

Designer:
Zaha Hadid Architects

At the Hungerberg station, one of four stations in Innsbruck, Austria, the architect Zaha Hadid has used state-of-the-art computer modelling to design double-curvature, thermoformed glass panels that are created in a three-dimensional mould.

The resulting shells (supported on a steel-rib structure) are intended to work with the contours and topography of the surrounding mountains. The panels are painted on the inside. The white glass, with its hard, reflective qualities and undulating forms serves not only its function as a railway station but also to create an artificial landscape that is reminiscent of the natural phenomena that is all around.

Again, as we have seen throughout this chapter, the creative potential of a material such as glass moves hand-in-hand with the progress of technological processes, such as computer modelling and manufacturing techniques. However, the inherent qualities of glass – its reactions to light – are never lost and are always exploited.

Above:
Computer render of the final design.

Below:
Section of the station.

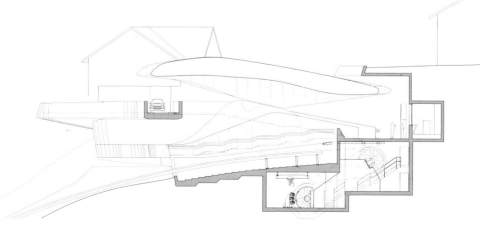

'Each station has its own unique context, topography, altitude, and circulation. We studied natural phenomena such as glacial moraines and ice movements – as we wanted each station to use the fluid language of natural ice formations, like a frozen stream on the mountainside.'

Zaha Hadid

Below:
Interior showing the use of double-curvature, thermoformed glass cladding.

Plastics

Seen as a wonder material, heralding the dawn of a new age of industrial design or, alternately, as vulgar and kitsch, cheap and disposable, the epitome of bad taste and the emblem of the throwaway society. Plastics arrived very late in the day when compared to the other materials that we have looked at so far, but their effect on design, on society and on the environment have been more dramatic and far-reaching than probably any other material in everyday use.

Capable of being shaped or moulded into a huge variety of objects and products, surfaces and finishes, plastics are everywhere. A material that is so ubiquitous, of infinite form, colour and texture. Objects and products, surfaces and finishes, that we cannot imagine living without, have all been designed and produced using techniques and innovations that started with the application of rubber gum to cotton by Macintosh in 1823 – and the waterproof 'mac' was born.

Name:
The Elastic Plastic Sponge at
The Coachella Valley Music
and Arts Festival

Location:
Indio, USA

Date:
2009

Designer:
Ball-Nogues Studio

The Elastic Plastic Sponge is
a large-scale installation made
from recycled plastic that can
be twisted, arched and curled
to form different types of space,
including a lounge, a theatre, or
a large, sculptural Mobius strip.

Plastics are made up of polymers: large molecules of elements such as carbon, hydrogen, oxygen, chlorine and fluorine that come together in long chains. The chemical combination of elements, and the molecular structures that these result in, enable a very wide range of plastics to be produced. Each different plastic has distinct qualities and limitations that lend themselves to specific applications across an ever-increasing variety of industries and design disciplines.

Late-nineteenth and early-twentieth centuries

What is less well known is that natural polymers have been with us, and used by us, for many thousands of years. The Worshipful Company of Horners, one of the ancient guild and livery companies of the City of London, is first recorded in 1284. Dedicated to the protection and promotion of the craft of using natural animal horn, the craft predates their official incorporation by many hundreds of years. Today the company is still very active, but due to the changing fashion in the use of horn – and the growth of plastics since the mid-nineteenth century – their activities today centre around working closely with the contemporary plastics industry.

Changing tastes and fashions have had a dramatic effect on the fortunes of plastic as an everyday material since production techniques were first established and patented in the late 1880s. Trying to find an artificial replacement for the shellac resin that was made from beetles, Dr Leo Baekeland developed Bakelite between 1907 and 1909.

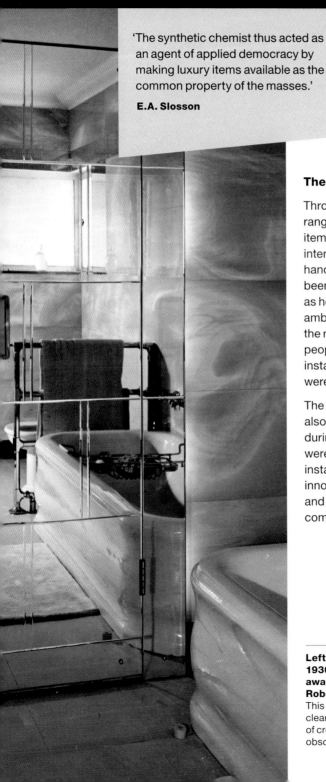

'The synthetic chemist thus acted as an agent of applied democracy by making luxury items available as the common property of the masses.'
E.A. Slosson

The interwar years

Through the 1920s and 1930s, a small range of plastics were used to produce items (jewellery, toys, decorative items and interior fittings such as bowls, cups, knobs, handles and lamps) that had previously been made from expensive materials such as horn, ivory, ebony, alabaster, onyx and amber. Whilst generally unaware of how the new 'wonder' material was produced, people from all sections of society were instantly aware of the impact that plastics were having on their quality of life.

The active marketing of plastics was also seen as a way of revitalizing industry during the post-war depression: they were well-finished, quick to produce, instantly functional and aesthetically innovative. Plastic democratized design and consumerism – plastics became commercially and socially acceptable.

Left:
1930s art deco
award-winning bathroom,
Robert W Symonds
This bathroom had walls lined in clear marbled marmorean, a floor of cream rubber and thermolux obscured glass in the windows.

History and context > International icons

Post-World War II

The mass-production of objects using and exploring these new materials was one of the key influences in the 'standardization' of the interior by modernist designers such as Le Corbusier. Understanding that objects and furniture had to be accommodated in an otherwise purist environment, interiors were intended to be reproduced and replicated just like the 'equipment' that formed part of the decorative scheme. However, in Britain, much of the public was suspicious of plastics that had successfully played such an important role in the war effort, and the desired return to normality was linked with the re-appropriation of 'natural' materials and the rejection of those seen to be 'imitation'.

However, the design industry pursued the modernist aesthetic that created a contemporary, domestic style based on lightness, variation, colour and pattern using new materials such as aluminium and plastics. Designers such as Charles and Ray Eames and manufacturers and retailers such as Heals sought to bring high-quality design in easy-to-produce and affordable materials to the optimism of 1950s society.

Facing page:
The Red Sun Pavilion at the Serpentine Gallery, London, UK, by Jean Nouvel, 2010
Red polycarbonate sheets and fabric structures provide a temporary but dramatic contrast to the traditional parkland setting of the gallery.

Much of the marketing was directed at women, who, being seen as the traditional homemaker of the time, were also seen as the chief consumer of the household. As portrayed in advertising, the domestic kitchen of the 1950s saw the housewife take pride of place surrounded by new appliances and gleaming, hygienic, plastic-coated furnishings and work surfaces. Women could exercise 'good taste' by choosing well-designed, efficient and useful products.

With the explosion of the consumerist, throwaway pop culture of the 1960s, the opportunities for plastics came into their own. Interior design moved to keep up with the rapidly changing fashions that were dominated by European youth. Music, art, fashion and the space race pushed design into evermore abstract and organic forms, well suited to the possibilities provided by developments in plastics materials and manufacture. Synthetic and cheap became glamorous and desirable.

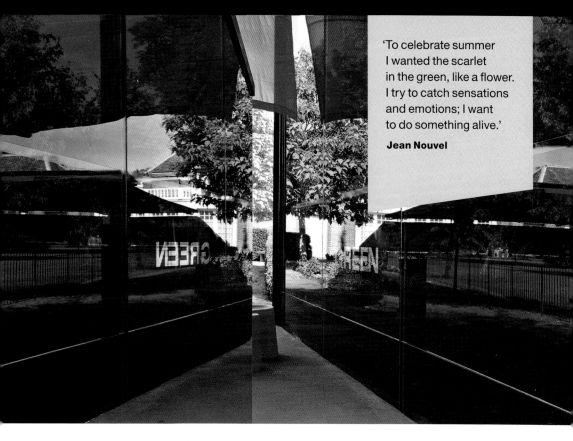

Today

There is no doubt that plastics have far exceeded the potential that their original inventors foresaw. Plastics such as polyethylene terephthalate (PET) provide us with the opportunity to experiment with forms and shapes that are unrealizable in any other type of material.

Plastics create lightweight but strong panels (at home in architectural, marine and aerospatial environments), capitalizing on the ability to organize and dictate the molecular structure of the material.

**Discussion point:
Plastics today**

It is hard to imagine life today without plastic. Look around your living or working environment.

● How many objects or elements are made from plastic?

● What materials do you think these would have been made from before plastics were widely available?

History and context > International icons

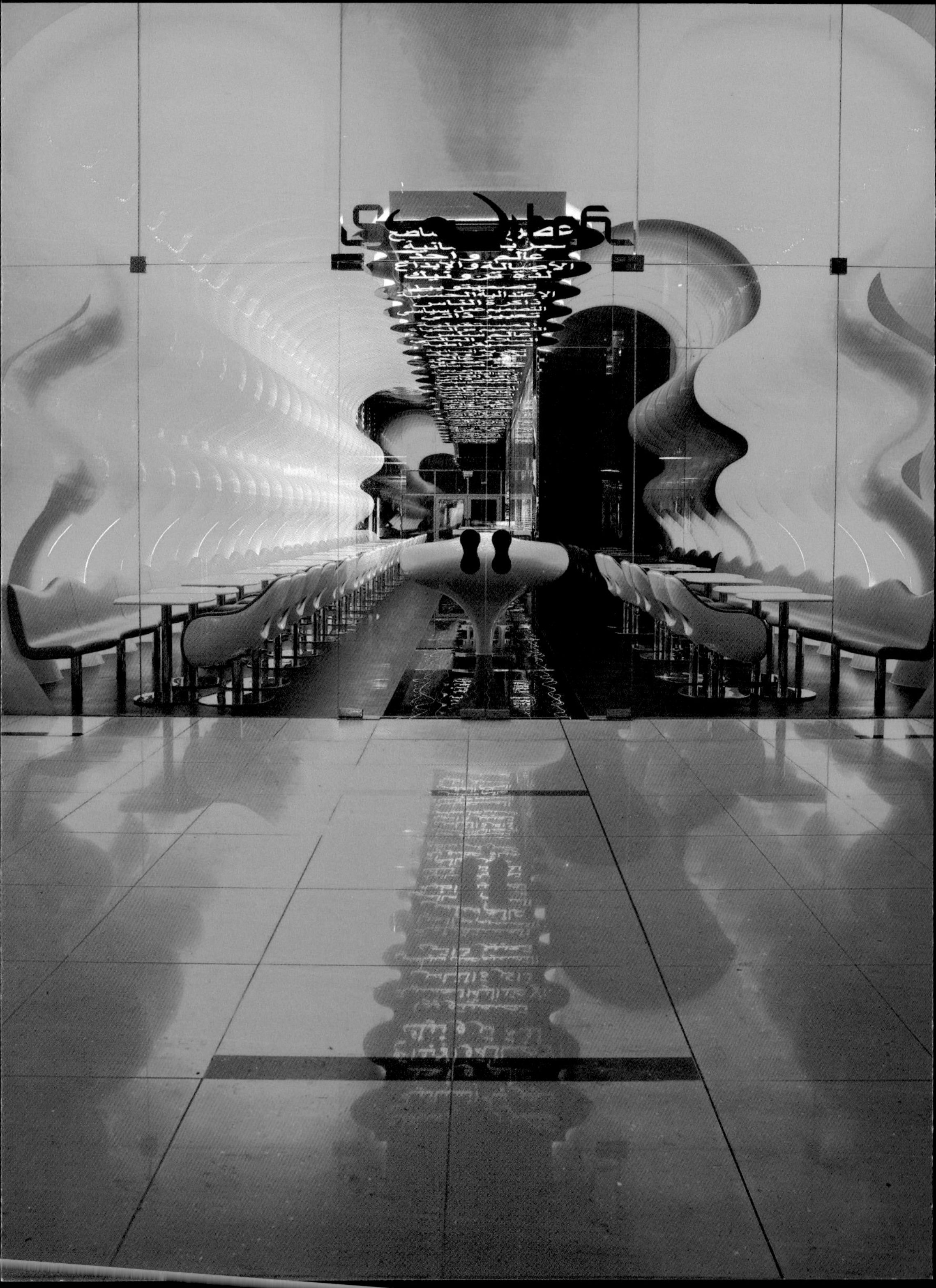

'I wanted Switch to be a strong, symmetrical, soft organic womblike space composed of a continuous, undulating wall that wraps around the entire restaurant.'

Karim Rashid

Previous spread:
The Disney Store Headquarters, Pasadena, USA, by Clive Wilkinson Architects, 2007
Rotation-moulded thin-walled polyethylene honeycombs tessellate to provide a private and sound-absorbing workspace that can be assembled, and disassembled by the users of the space. This brings play into the workplace and allows the employees to take control of their environment.

Facing page:
Switch Restaurant, Dubai, UAE, by Karim Rashid, 2009
The undulating plastic of the interior communicates the individualism of the restaurant and the dune landscape of the location.

Types of plastic

Polyester films let us see the inner workings of our bodies, allow us to sail around the world and even let us print the money that keeps the world at work.

Polypropylene contains our medical and nutritional requirements, keeping them sterile.

Thermochromic plastics allow us to see if a baby's milk is too hot.

High-density polyethylene fibre (HDPE) provides the fabric that can protect us in harsh environments.

Nylon provides much of the gearing that keeps our cars on the road.

Shock-absorbing foams (SAFs) send us comfortably to sleep at night.

In short, all of these plastic materials, and many, many, more that have not been mentioned, have made our lives in the twenty-first century what they are – just look around you and think how cold, draughty, noisy and dark your own homes would be without the intervention of plastics.

As we have seen in this chapter, plastics have come a long way since their invention and production at the beginning of the twentieth century. However, for much of that time their use has been limited to the manufacture of object-based products and smaller elements of the construction process. Plastics as the main driver behind interior architecture and interior design has been a relatively recent development. The case studies shown here concentrate on the innovative use of plastic to create an interior space and atmosphere that could not have been created with any other type of material.

Facing page:
The interior is made up of 60,000 transparent 7.5-metre-long acrylic, optical strands, each containing a seed. The interior is silent and illuminated only by the daylight that has filtered past each seed through each optical hair.

Below:
Sixty thousand seeds will be dispersed across the UK and China at the end of the expo.

Heatherwick Studio

Name:
Seed Cathedral

Location:
UK Pavilion at the Shanghai Expo

Date:
2010

Designer:
Heatherwick Studio

With the theme of the World Expo 2010 Shanghai being 'Better City, Better Life', the Seed Cathedral by Heatherwick Studio, in conjunction with the multi-layered, 6,000 m² landscape on which it sits, is intended to showcase the work of the Royal Botanical Gardens at Kew and their Millennium Seedbank.

Each individually positioned acrylic optical strand, making up the interior of the pavilion, contains a seed in its tip. In a further connection with the ecological work of Kew, Heatherwick asserted that all the seeds used in the pavilion must have been found within 300 km (approximately 185 miles) of the expo site: China's Kunming Institute of Botany, a partner of Kew on the Seedbank project, donated the seeds. Inspired by fields of crops blowing in the wind, the acrylic rods are free to sway gently when the wind blows across the site. At night, the rods are softly illuminated by fibre-optic elements encased in each and the whole is reminiscent of a dandelion turned to seed.

At the end of the expo, each of the 60,000 rods is to be 'blown' across schools in Britain and China to not only provide an inspirational memento of the project but also a symbolic tie between the two countries.

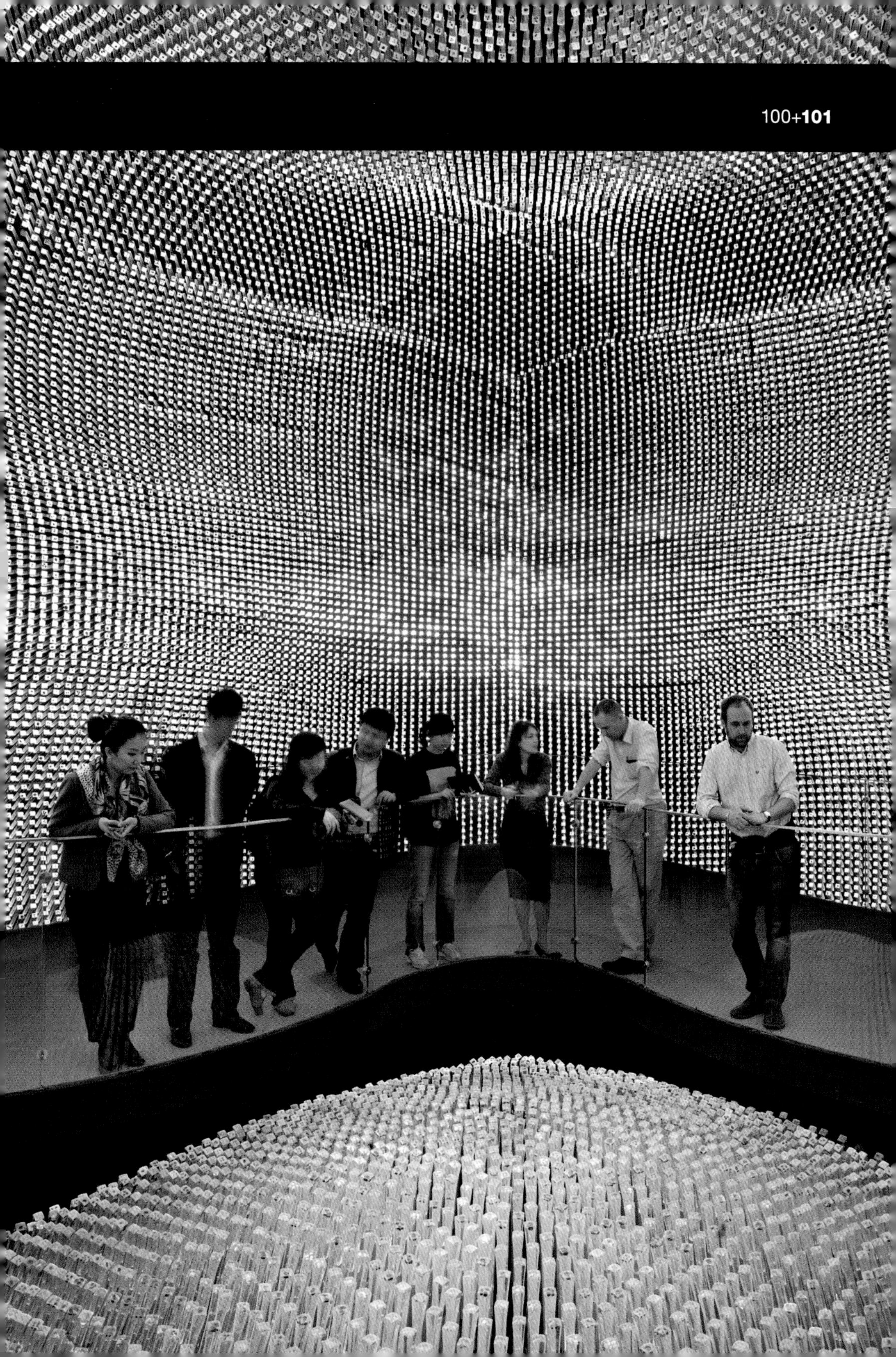

Left:
The counter gently hovers and
is the literal location providing
the medicinal means to recovery
and relief.

Below:
Plastics have been shaped
and moulded to create a flowing,
organic space.

Right:
Floor plan of pharmacy.

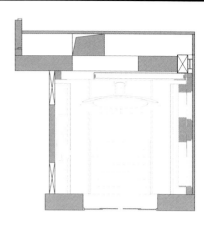

Karim Rashid

Name:
Oaza Zdravlja Pharmacy

Location:
Belgrade, Serbia

Date:
2009

Designer:
Karim Rashid

In the design of this space, Rashid has exemplified the opportunities of plastics and their manufacture, driven by digital design, to create a bold and expressive yet simple and flowing interior. If we consider the qualities of plastics that have been discussed in this chapter (colour, form and texture) we see here that Rashid is adept at bringing all of these to play to stimulate a contemporary audience and provide a contemporary, 'visual and info-aware' experience.

As Rashid explains, 'Through the use of soft flowing walls and organic shapes a sense of comfort and security is immediately established. Framed by the sweeping curvature of the walls, a simple, yet powerful counter elegantly hovers above the ground plane. This form is symbolic of the journey medication takes through the body's cellular framework'.

The potential for plastics to be shaped and moulded has allowed Rashid to create spaces and zones that reference the human body and its intricate healing process.

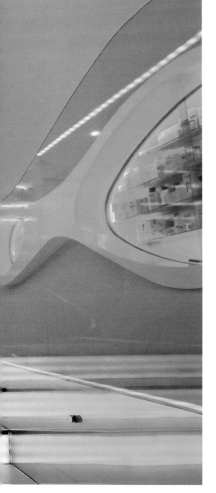

Below:
Simple polystyrene has been used here to create an innovative shelving unit and spatial divider.

Facing page:
The simplicity of the 'Clouds' system allows the user to structure and design their own interior space.

Clouds modular shelving system

Name:
'Clouds', for Cappellini

Location:
N/A

Date:
2002

Designer:
Ronan and Erwan Bouroullec

For over ten years the work of the Bouroullecs has been characterized by the innovative use of plastics and textiles to produce contemporary products, industrial design, architecture and interiors for some of the world's leading manufacturers and designers: Vitra, Kvadrat, Magis, Kartell, Established and Sons, Ligne Roset, Axor, Alessi, Issey Miyake and Cappellini and Camper.

As Ronan Bouroullec explains, 'our work is deeply tied to simplicity. Few people understand to what extent doing something simple is an extremely complicated thing, I am not talking about simplicity as a style I am talking about the fact that when a project is different and is good its something extremely complicated. So it comes into being through the process of doing, in fact, and redoing and redoing and redoing and redoing and refining and refining and refining. It requires collective intelligence, and design is really about that, it's really about collective intelligence.'

Inspiration from nature and the structures found in nature are translated through the use of unnatural materials into the industrial and urban context.

Here, a material as banal as polystyrene has been redesigned and manufactured to produce a free-standing shelving unit that also acts as a spatial divider. The beauty of the design relies on its simplicity, visual and physical lightness and self-assembly without the need for skilled labour.

The experimentation of the Bouroullecs has succeeded in combining the functional qualities of a type of material that is often seen as being disposable and lacking in honesty with the individualism of installation art: 'The Clouds help you design space as you wish. They divide up space. They can focus on a specific area, or a wall, they can make a mark, give space direction, a front and a back. This is one aspect. And the other aspect is that the Clouds can give structure to spaces. In the case of living space they can separate different areas, purely psychologically, without putting up new walls or converting the house, which in most cases is not possible. In other cases they can cover walls and, given their soft material, enable different physical sensations. It is important for working and living areas to be made humane with aids such as these.'

As mentioned at the start of this chapter, plastics – in all their hundreds of varieties – have probably raised more social and environmental issues than any other material in everyday use. They have provided us with the opportunity to bring functional and aesthetic quality to our lives at a price that is affordable by all. The low, personal, economic costs associated with their use has been key to their success but the high cost to the environment is only recently beginning to be understood.

According to both the British Plastics Federation and the Plastics Industry Trade Association of America, the construction industry is the second biggest consumer of plastics, after the packaging industry. Used for seals, profiles (windows and doors), pipes, cables, floor coverings and insulation, plastics are light, easily formed and require minimum maintenance. They also require energy-intensive processes for manufacture and rely on the use of highly toxic chemicals, such as chlorine, in their design (according to Greenpeace over 56 per cent of the weight of raw PVC is chlorine with the rest being products synthesized from oil).

With so much of the plastics in construction being incorporated into the production of a building – and so remaining largely unseen – it would be understandable to question where the assertions of the BPF come from. However, if you look around the cities and towns of the UK, Europe and North America the reason soon becomes obvious: PVC windows and doors.

Using PVC in doors and windows can cost the building owner one third that of using timber. With a useable service life of less than 20 years and problems inherent in the recycling or incineration of PVC products (with the release of those chemical constituents present in the manufacturing process), it is debatable whether the short-term benefits delivered to our comfortable living and working environments will be outweighed by the long-term damage to our ecosystems.

Interior and architectural designers around the world are grappling with the opportunities and limitations of the responsible reuse of materials. True, recycling itself often requires the use of significant energy and toxic chemical processes (as in the case of polar fleece and its manufacture from recycled plastic drinks bottles). Things that are produced using plastics are often inherently designed to fulfil specific functions and are not easily reused in a different context. Plastic will be with us for many years to come but the products produced, and discarded, will be with us for far longer.

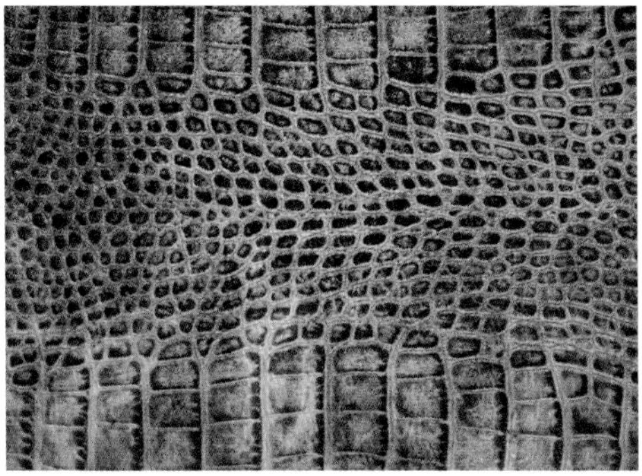
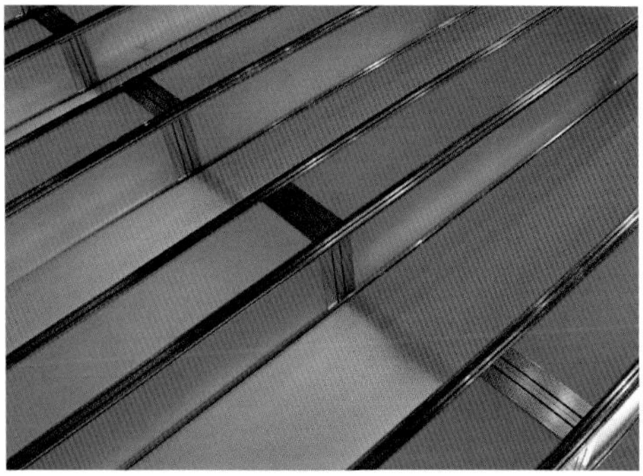

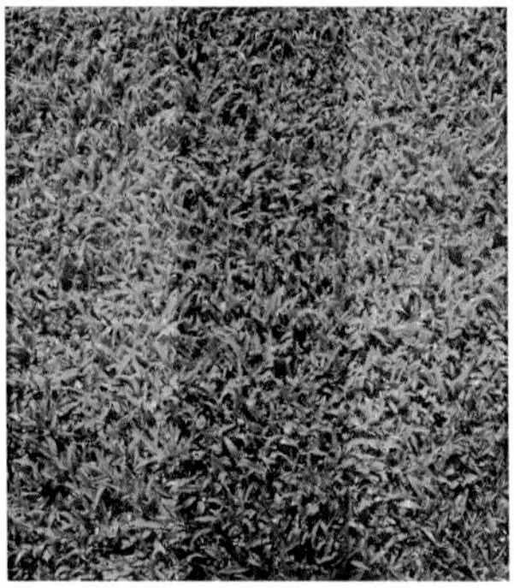
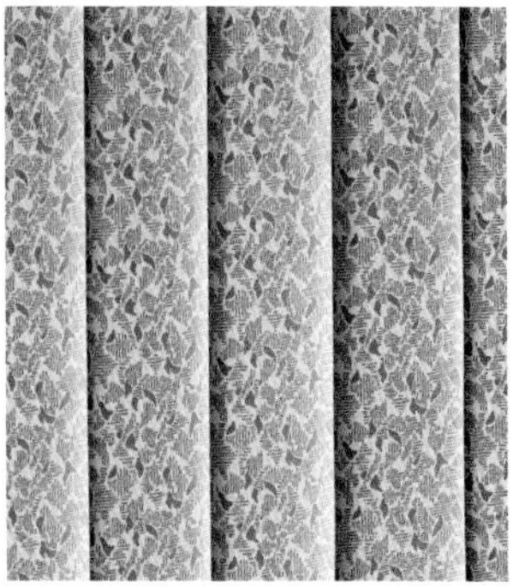
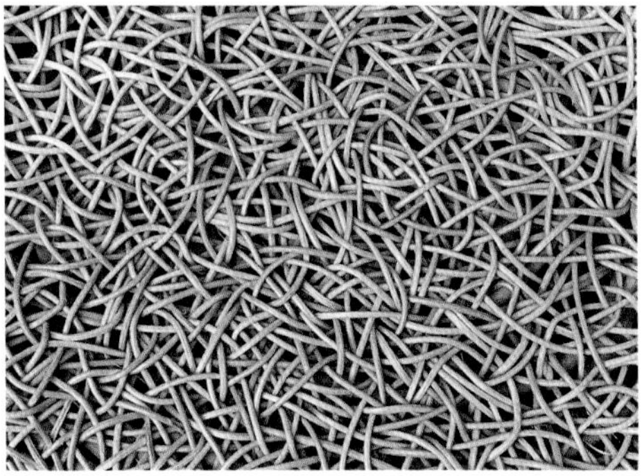
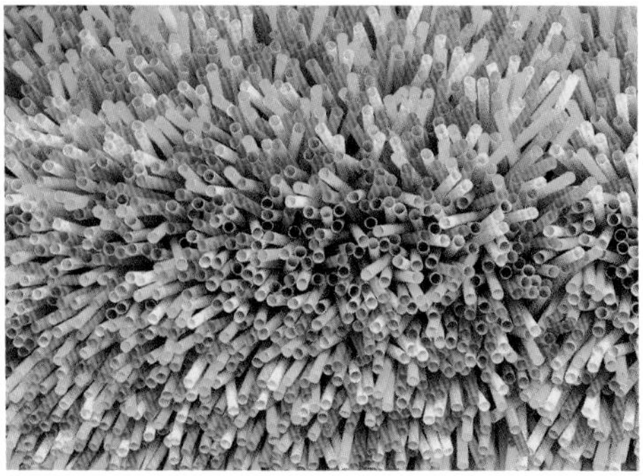
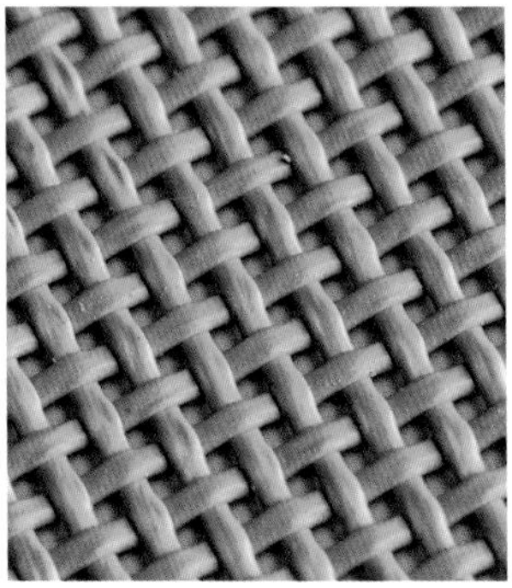
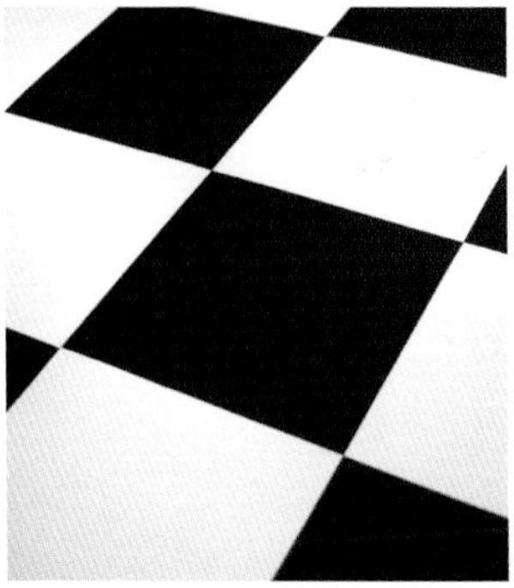
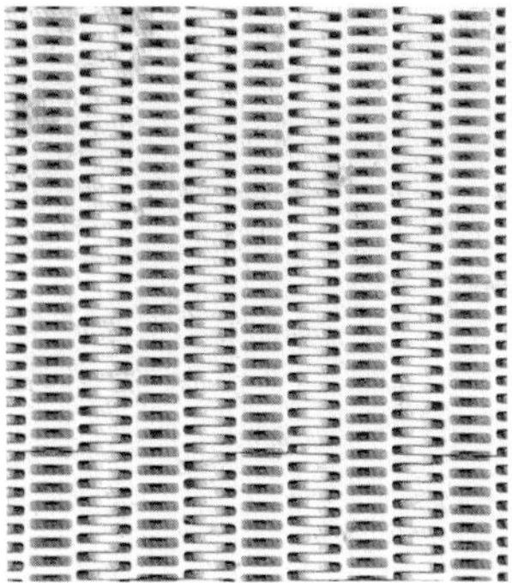

Clearly plastics will continue to be used across all design disciplines. The responsible use of these controversial materials is the responsibility of interior, architectural, product and industrial designers. The project detailed here illustrates and demonstrates that efforts can be made to produce innovative and exciting environments whilst making the most efficient, ecological use of the materials we have.

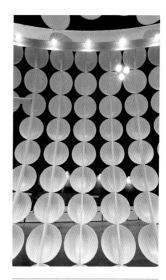

The Plasticamente Pavilion

Name:
The Plasticamente Pavilion

Location:
Travelling exhibition

Date:
2008

Designer:
Riccardo Giovanetti

Using recycled plastic as the vehicle to promote a film and exhibition about recycling was the directive behind the commissioning of this travelling pavilion. Intended to allow for the exploration of the qualities of plastic and other recyclables, it has been designed using 130 m² of white plastic discs that reference the molecular composition of the polymers that it exhibits.

As the architect explains, 'Although this is a large pavilion it gives an impression of weightlessness, and can appear almost animate and breathing. The pavilion's exterior develops into a rich variety of interior point of views that maximize the potential to reuse and rethink space due to the innate flexibility of its plan.'

Above:
The pavilion is made up of 130 m² of white plastic discs.

Facing page top:
The pavilion was commissioned by the Italian Institute of Recycled Plastic.

Facing page bottom:
The interior space is designed as a covered precinct for visitors to rest in and live the film experience.

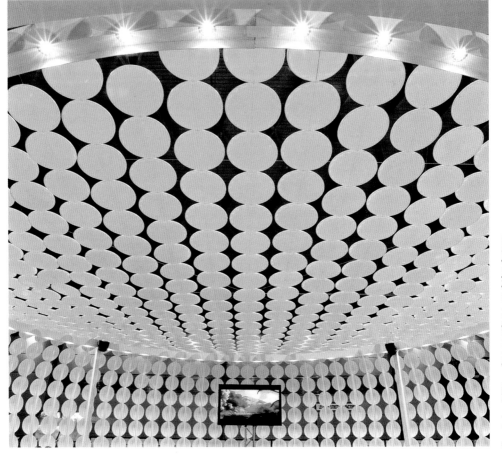

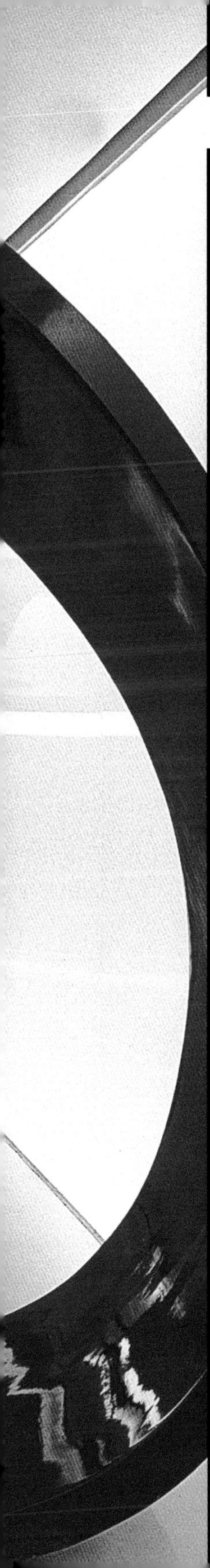

Composites are those materials that are made up of a variety of constituent parts or elements. We have already seen their use in other chapters, for instance when looking at wood we saw the development of plywood at the end of the nineteenth century and its extensive use in early twentieth-century modernist designs. It is probably fair to say that in the context of interior architecture and design today the term 'composite' describes a range of materials that are at the cutting edge of contemporary design and that demonstrate the exceptional creativity of some of our finest designers. Creativity will be the focus of this chapter rather than the technicalities of how these materials are manufactured, but it should be stressed that the opportunity to realize the often dramatic and visually complex designs that we will look at has not come about without the combined knowledge and expertise of designers and manufacturers alike.

Name:
Emporio Armani,
Chater House Project

Location:
Hong Kong

Date:
2002

Designer:
Doriana and Massimiliano
Fuksas Architects

The 'red ribbon' created out of fibreglass emphasizes 'tension and meaning' and 'builds' space within the store.

Although the use of materials made up of constituent parts has been in evidence since classical times (remember that the Romans used concrete), their use as materials in their own right to create design has been limited until the technological advances of the twentieth century. Today these materials can make use of traditional elements combined with contemporary agents. For example, medium-density fibreboard, or MDF (sometimes called milled wood composite) involves breaking hard or soft wood waste products into their basic fibres and then combining them with wax and resin under high temperatures and pressures to create a dense board.

Composites can also make use of new materials technology to create innovative products that allow opportunities for experimental design. Fibreglass, or glass-reinforced plastic (GRP) is, as the name suggests, a material using fine fibres of glass held together in a matrix by the addition of a resin and a hardener; first used in boat building in the 1950s, it has since begun to replace metals in the construction of yachts and aircraft. It has itself progressively been replaced by carbon-fibre reinforced plastics (CFRP), which are stronger and lighter than their glass predecessor – but also far more expensive.

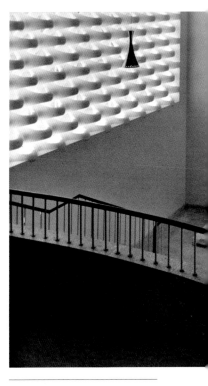

Above:
'Continua' architectural
screen by Erwin Hauer, 1950
Interested in the exploration of infinite, continuous surfaces, Hauer developed his modular screens from a variety of composite materials such as milled wood composite (MDF), milled stone, cast gypsum and cast cement.

Composites

Contemporary design

Composites today are, by their nature, usually very lightweight and very strong. This allows them to be used to create dynamic forms that can be self-supporting and which do not rely on structural support from the surrounding space. Using construction methods such as those outlined on the previous page, (GRP and CFRP) designers have become liberated from the restrictions in form and space that were inherently imposed by conventional, modular, angular building materials. Today, ideas of movement and flow through a space, previously negotiated through the plan, the section and elements placed within them, can be expressed in continuous, fluid forms that give a dynamic and dramatic, weaving and tying together of spaces as never before. In some of the examples that will be considered later, it is the composite form that makes the interior and creates the space – the 'box' that these interventions sit within is of lesser importance and has often been designed to set the stage for its contrasting counterpart.

In exhibiting products, the use of these materials can begin to express and enhance the very nature of the brand itself, whether this is technology and precision or speed and style.

Modernism

Without repeating material that has already been covered in earlier chapters, it is worth reminding ourselves of perhaps the most widespread composite material and the one that defined the modernist movement in design: concrete. As a composite of sand, cement, aggregates and water, a broken piece of concrete will illustrate, perhaps more clearly than any other, the nature of composites. Take a close look and you will be able to see how each of the constituent elements are still visible in their original forms; only the cement, which has chemically combined with the water, has changed its state but its fine, granular, particles might still be discernable.

Composites

**Maserati Showroom HQ,
Modena, Italy, by Ron Arad,
2002–2003**
The intricate structure of
the 'loop' is itself an element
of precision engineering that
reflects the technological
excellence of the product being
displayed; the dynamic sweep
reflects the dynamism of the car.

Composites today

The possibilities of manufacture also allow for the communication of more abstract qualities of brand and culture through the use of motifs and light.

Developments in design and technology have not just favoured those materials that might be thought of as being 'high-tech'. Materials that might be considered primitive and the bastion of traditional interior design, such as paper, card and textiles, have drawn from innovations in composites to create spaces that are experimental in their context and form but are still fundamentally dictated by the tectonic qualities of the material being used, such as folding, pleating, wrapping and weaving.

The very language used to describe such spaces demonstrates how the use of these new materials is blurring the boundaries between different design disciplines, such as interior architecture, fashion and textile design.

Above:
'Leafy Shade', entrance hall to office building, Shanghai, China, by A-Asterisk Design Shanghai, 2008
This project includes the use of glass-fibre-reinforced gypsum with a bamboo motif to reflect the cultural taste of the client.

Although relatively recent in terms of design history, composite materials have provided modern and contemporary interior architects with the opportunity to create some of the most innovative and expressive forms. The work considered here exemplifies the opportunities that composites bring in the radical approach that has been taken to material technology, manufacturing processes and design. What results are dramatic interior designs that not only represent the historical scope of composites but also guarantee their future development.

Below:
Cast gypsum (hydrostone).

Facing page:
Detail, lit from behind.

'I cannot manipulate light;
I manipulate shape. The light's
a given, the shape is not.'

Erwin Hauer

Erwin Hauer

Name:
Knoll Internacional de Mexico
showroom

Location:
Mexico City

Date:
1961

Designer:
Erwin Hauer

With the appearance of 'Design 1' in 1950 (shown here installed in Knoll Internacional de Mexico showroom in Mexico City), the sculptor Erwin Hauer instantly stamped his presence on modernism. Cast in gypsum, or 'hydrostone', the screen elements took their inspiration from the 'saddle surfaces' of Henry Moore where the 'closure of form' is prevented but instead contain 'the seed of infinite expansion and, when used as a module, continues to expand while it goes through repeating convoluted configurations.'

Erwin Hauer explains, 'Continuity and potential infinity have been at the very centre of my sculpture from early on. I derived the notion of a continuous surface primarily from my studies of biomorphic form. This was greatly reinforced by my first encounter with the works of Henry Moore, who combined the dominant continuity of surface with an unprecedented cultivation of interior spaces within his sculpture.'

Unrelenting in their whiteness and purity and dominated by the use of cast stone composite, cast concrete and milled stone, the infinite forms of Hauer were the perfect opportunity for modernist design to accentuate the relationship between form and light – perhaps the key principle behind the movement. Coining the term 'modular constructivism', such sculptures were characterized by the careful use of intricate, and often infinite, repeating patterns that create potentially limitless planes and screens.

Above:
Physical 'chewing gum' connecting the spaces of the Moore Building.

Left and facing page:
Computer modelling showing the intentions of the design.

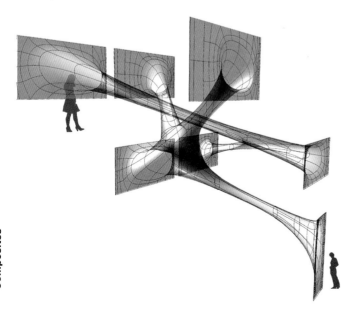

Composites

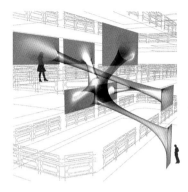

'Many people say my works are too complicated. But it is similar to nature which is also complex… but there is also order and organization in nature, just like in my works.'

Zaha Hadid

Zaha Hadid

Name:
Elastika at Design.05,
Art Basel

Location:
Miami, USA

Date:
2005

Designer:
Zaha Hadid

If the work of Hauer typified modernist interiors then the work of Hadid has certainly defined the opportunities that innovative materials and technology bring to contemporary design. Combining the use of composites with exceptional creativity in the use of computing and digital machinery, Hadid has succeeded in redefining the nature of interior space.

As an installation in the existing Moore Building (built in 1921), Hadid attempts to link the horizontal circulation with the dominant vertical columns that stretch across four stories. By creating a 'chewing gum' effect, the intention is to span the spaces and establish an 'elastic/plastic' connection between the floors.

Like so many of the works and materials that have been considered in this book, such innovation has only been possible when developments in materials technology have been married with developments in modelling and manufacturing techniques. Hadid's work manages to realize this marriage whilst at the same time generating forms of such grace and beauty that it can be easy to forget the complex processes that have been undertaken in their creation.

Like so many of the projects and materials that we have considered in this book, the question of the sustainability of composites is largely dependent on your particular view of this term and how you are able to apply your view to the discipline in which you practice. It could be argued that many composite materials make efficient use of constituent parts and often waste products from other, more conventional manufacturing processes: MDF uses waste wood fibres to create heard-wearing board and forms. However, it would be foolish to pretend that the manufacture of many of these products does not in itself rely on high levels of energy usage and the combination of environmentally unfriendly adhesives, resins and solvents.

Many composite materials, whether we look at concrete or glass and carbon fibre technologies, are difficult to reuse once they have been formed (even concrete can only realistically be reused for groundfill and compaction).

It would be fair to say that the advantage of using these materials, especially when linked with current modelling and geometrical software, is that we are able to produce the maximum structural performance with the minimum use of material – at least allowing for vastly improved efficiency in what we choose to use.

Many designers and their clients are attempting to promote a more ethical approach to projects and the use of resources.

As an example, we could consider the approach taken by one of the world's largest car manufacturers: Volkswagen. Since 31 May 2000, the Autostadt complex has attempted not only to engage the community with the brand and their products, but also to focus on the ethical and sustainable philosophies of the company. As part of this, Volkswagen have engaged artists and designers in the installation of a permanent exhibition called 'Level Green – The Concept of Sustainability'.

The architect of the exhibition, Jürgen Mayer, has allowed the philosophy behind the exhibition to drive the concept, design and themed areas that it contains. The increasingly complex sections are all produced in easily processed and reusable MDF, each containing a supporting steel structure that is bolted to the floor.

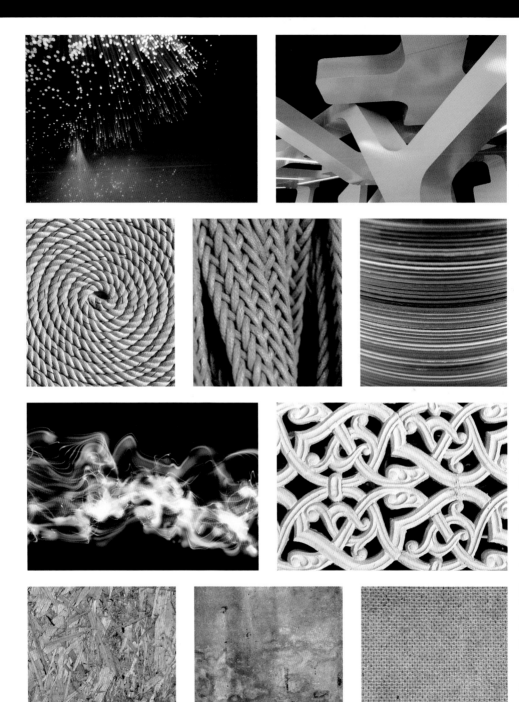

The development of new composite materials and new manufacturing and production techniques is leading the way in the creation of dynamic interior spaces and installations. Computer three-dimensional modelling software packages, when combined with three-dimensional printing technology and CNC cutting, are allowing designers to model and then construct dramatic forms that have never been possible before. Highly efficient three-dimensional spaces and structures make use of the minimum amount of material; traditional representations of design have been re-appropriated and transformed by technology into exciting, contemporary objects.

Above:
Thermoformed Corian composite with CNC applied engraved pattern.

Tablecloth

Name:
Tablecloth for Fortnum & Mason

Location:
Heathrow Airport

Date:
2005

Designer:
Brinkworth Design Ltd

The Fortnum and Mason tablecloth by Brinkworth Design took the most familiar of domestic objects and transformed it, using the thermoformed composite Corian and CNC engraving (to create embroidery-like patterns on the surface), into an eye-catching and unique contemporary object.

Aperiodic Symmetries

Name:
Aperiodic Symmetries

Location:
University of Calgary

Date:
2009

Designer:
Marc Fornes and Theverymany

In interior spaces, as we have seen from the work of Fornes, Fuksas, Hauer, Hadid and Mayer, the architectural 'box' is now taking second place to the innovative elements that inhabit it, allowing designers to explore and visualize the subtleties of space as never before. Movement and flow that have, until now, been represented by the configuration of planes are now being expressed in the most fluid of forms.

Below:
Rhinoscript computation: 1,640 parts, 757 unique star connections, 883 panels (11 unique types), 5 days CNC cutting, 30 sheets 4 x 8' of ½"-thick polyethylene, 8 people, 72 hours assembly time.

Mention tiles and you would be forgiven for thinking of small square or rectangular pieces of ceramic stuck to the walls or floors of our houses. Since Roman times, tiles have been used to create durable and ornamental surfaces, both inside and outside our buildings.

However, the ability to break down complex patterns and designs into smaller, manageable units, or to apply thinner, cheaper layers of often expensive finishes onto a module (easily handled by a person), has ensured that tiles – in whatever material they are made – have remained one of the key materials in applying colour and texture to interior spaces.

This chapter will not only look at the, perhaps more recognizable, application of tiles in interior space, but also at situations where tiles are designed for specific technical reasons or where more unusual materials have been applied to create a tiled effect: the breaking down of scale or the repeating of a pattern.

Name:
Octavilla

Location:
Stockholm, Sweden

Date:
2009

Designer:
Elding Oscarson

Alteration, interior and design identity for a graphic design agency; the new wall is constructed of bundled magazines held in a steel cage, creating a tile effect.

For at least 2,000 years the artistic desire has been present, and the technical skills have been practised, to break down large and complicated designs into intricate pieces that can be assembled on the surfaces of our buildings. The provision of both durable and beautiful walls, floors and ceilings have driven the experimentation with tiles for all but the most recent of these times.

Classical times

The Romans used small sections of stone, glass and ceramic – or tessera – to depict scenes of social and religious importance as a form of applied decoration to their homes and public buildings. Often using materials that occurred locally, earlier designs were usually restricted to black and white representations of strong geometric patterns – the basis for these patterns can be traced back to mathematical systems far older, such as those found in ancient Sumer, Egypt and Greece.

It was not until the fourth century that high-quality, coloured, figurative designs depicting scenes of both everyday life and religious importance became commonplace.

Above:
Roman mosaic
Many Roman mosaics used strong geometric patterns such as this. Later, tiles were used to recreate images depicting religious scenes and everyday life.

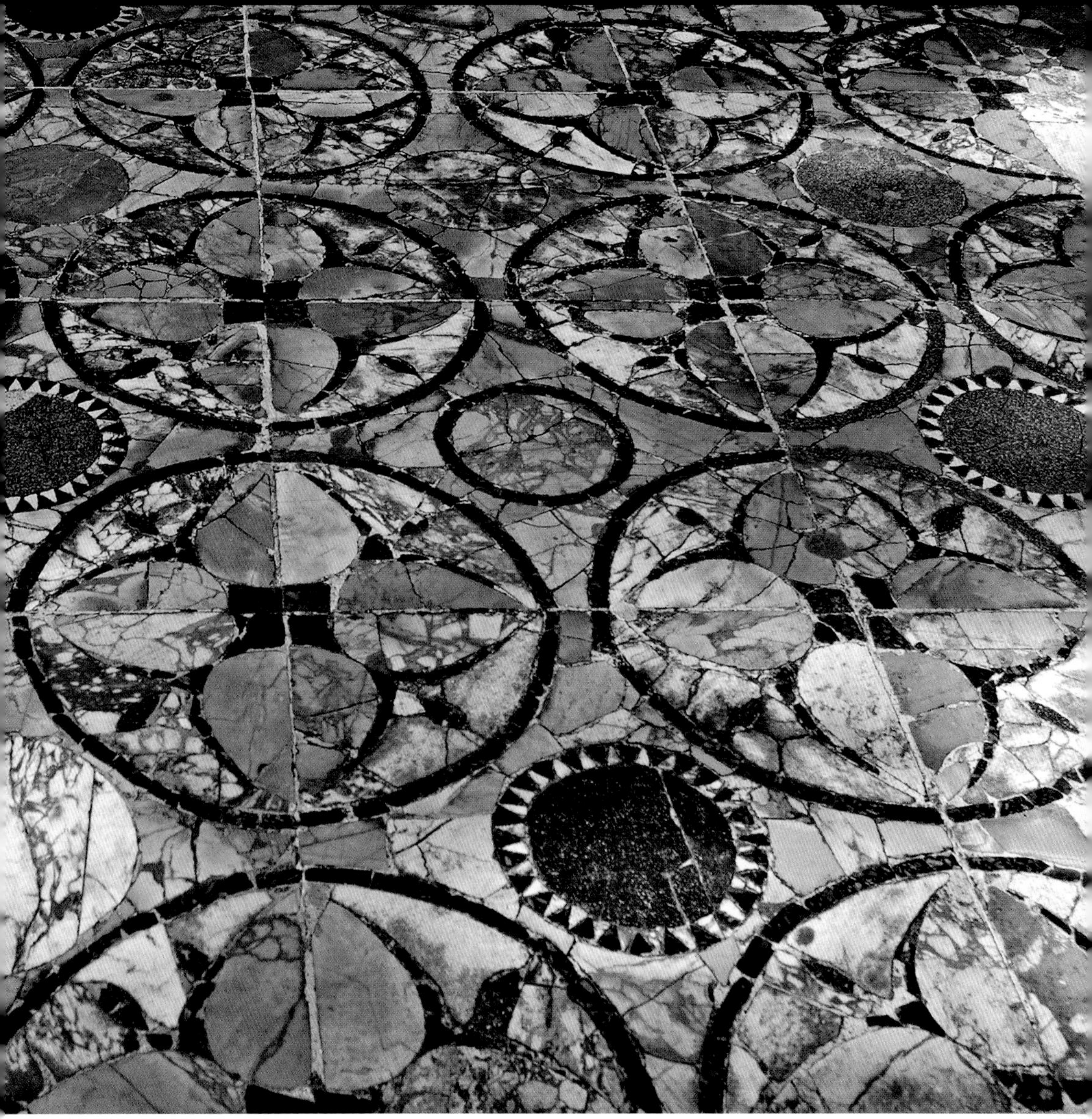

Medieval

Again demonstrating the opportunity for expensive finishes to be applied to an interior surface as a tile, mosaics featured strongly in the medieval decoration of the early Christian basilicas and cathedrals. Most likely leading on from their use as a Roman art form, and appropriated as the Roman Empire adopted Christianity as its central faith, medieval cathedrals were solely concerned with depicting and reinforcing the message of the Gospels.

Above:
San Giusto Cathedral,
Trieste, Italy,
twelfth–thirteenth centuries
Apsidal mosaics draw attention to the altar.

The focus of the delivery of this message was the altar and the architecture of the building reflected this with a dome or spire being positioned above. Inside, this was further emphasized by the use of apsidal mosaics to draw the gaze and provide suitable grandeur and illumination.

Renaissance, baroque and rococo

Distinct in their difference from mosaics
(where many small elements are used
to create a design rather than a tile, which
often has the design painted or applied to it),
the early use of tiles became synonymous
with many cultures around the world.
Introduced by North African cultures to
Spain and Portugal in the fifteenth century,
azulejos, (deriving from the Arabic term for
polished stone) were often used to depict
mythological or biblical scenes.

Characteristically produced in blue and
white, they were used on a large scale
to decorate the interior and exterior
façades of many churches, the exuberance
of the decoration matched only by the
architectural excess of the period. They
not only have a pronounced visual contrast
to the soft-coloured stone of the buildings
they adorn, almost making them feel
a much later addition than they are, but
they must also have given the interior
spaces a noticeably colder atmosphere
than the warming glow of the gold and
rich earthy tones of the medieval cathedral.

Below:
Tile work in Oporto
Cathedral, Portugal, by
Valentim de Almeida, 1731
Gothic cloister of the cathedral,
decorated with baroque *azulejos*
by Valentim de Almeida between
1729 and 1731.

Facing page:
Tile panel, by William Morris,
1834–96
Sixty-six slip-covered and
hand-painted earthenware tiles
come together to create a typical
Morris design.

Georgian, Regency and Victorian

Throughout the Georgian, Regency and
Victorian periods, tiles continued to be
used to create ornate yet durable interior
surfaces. Designs moved away from the
depiction of mythical or biblical scenes
and instead were used to apply rich colour
and pattern or, in keeping with the art
of the time, to paint a picture of idealized
scenes of everyday life. In the spirit of
the mass-production techniques of the
time, many large civic buildings such
as museums, universities and town halls
made use of elaborate terracotta tiles that
could be reproduced in large quantities,
and to accurate dimensions, from plaster
moulds. Resistant to the often corrosive
industrial atmosphere, the use of local
clays as well as the skills of the craftsman
enabled highly detailed tiles in both pattern
and relief to bring colour, texture and
narrative to many of the grandest buildings
that still exist in our cities today.

The aesthetic movements

In keeping with the return to craft-led
representation and design espoused by
those driving the Arts and Crafts movement,
tiles formed a central part of the decorative
techniques applied to the interior by key
figures such as Webb and Morris. Depicting
highly detailed and dense, naturalistic
designs, usually in deep colours coated
with rich glazes, tiles were often composed
as panels of individual pieces which, when
brought together, would create one overall
design. Several of these panels would
then form a larger composition, together
with wooden panelling, wallpaper and
silks. The effect must have been stunning –
if perhaps a little dark.

'What about the concrete block? It was the cheapest (and ugliest) thing in the building world. It lived mostly in the architectural gutter as an imitation of rock-faced stone. Why not see what could be done with that gutter rat? Steel rods cast inside the joints of the blocks themselves and the whole brought into some broad, practical scheme of general treatment, why would it not be fit for a new phase of our modern architecture? It might be permanent, noble beautiful.'

Frank Lloyd Wright

Modernism

As we have discussed earlier, the modernists were concerned with the purity of their architecture and the predominant use of glass, steel and concrete enabled the leading designers of the period to rationalize form, expose structure and banish ornament from their buildings. It is unusual to find any degree of decorative finishes in modernist buildings, except those by one of the leading lights of the time: Frank Lloyd Wright. Wright believed that his buildings should connect people with nature and that there should be a natural transition between the exterior and the interior – that barriers should dissolve. Fascinated by the opportunities of concrete as a construction material, and wanting to emphasize such a seamless transition, he used patterned concrete tiles to construct and decorate his 'textile block houses' (of which four were built between 1923 and 1924). Unmistakably Mayan in influence, the geometric patterns on the blocks not only resonate with this ancient civilization, perhaps giving a feel of place and permanence, but also serving to visually break up what could otherwise be a heavy exterior and interior finish.

Facing page:
The Ennis House,
Los Angeles, USA, by
Frank Lloyd Wright, 1924
An interior view of Wright's 'textile block' concrete tiles.

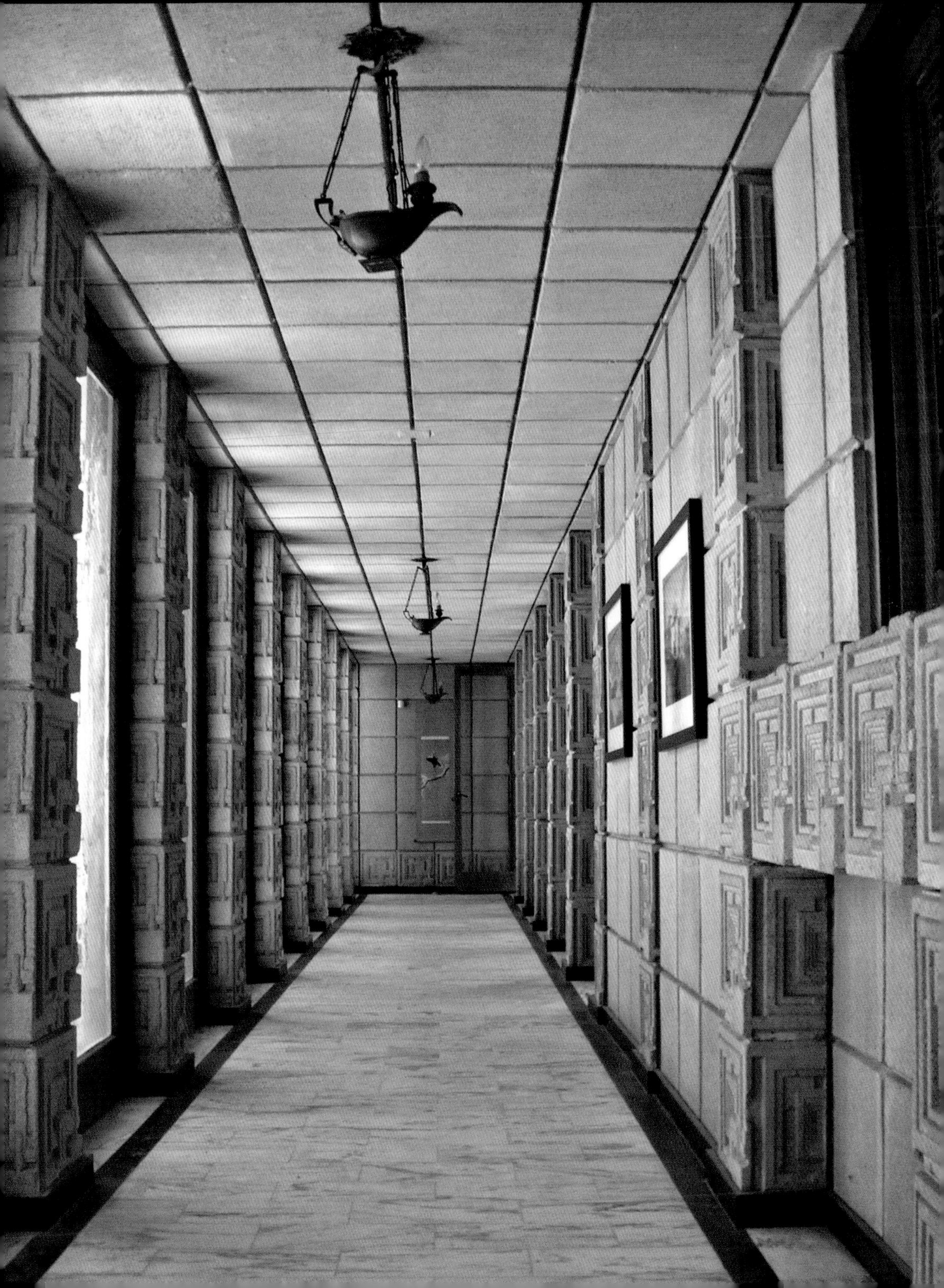

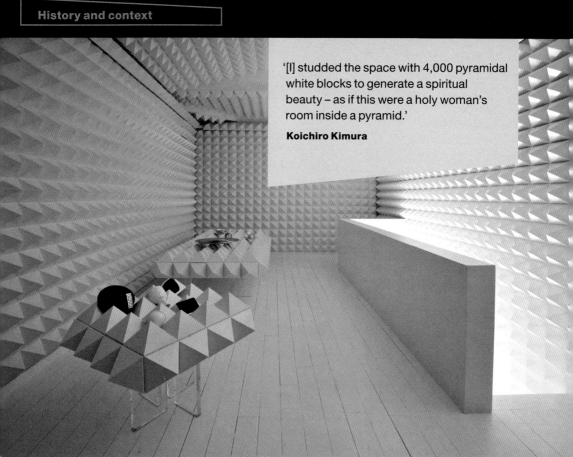

'[I] studded the space with 4,000 pyramidal white blocks to generate a spiritual beauty – as if this were a holy woman's room inside a pyramid.'

Koichiro Kimura

Above:
Koichiro Kimura Ayoama Showroom, Tokyo, Japan, by Koichiro Kimura, 2010
Four thousand white-lacquered pyramids, a signature form of the designer.

Facing page:
3142 Hoge Hotelschool, Maastricht, Netherlands, by Studio Makkink & Bey, 2010
A contemporary hotel bathroom.

Postmodern and contemporary

Today the potential of new materials in creating tiled effects has led to an abundant reinterpretation and reappropriation of a surface form that, as we have seen, has been around for thousands of years. Artists and designers are recreating the traditional setting of tiles in contemporary fashion.

The opportunity to apply conventional materials in unconventional contexts through the use of tiles allows texture and identity to be created in spaces where the communication of the message or brand of the client is essential.

Spiritual or mythological connotations are implied, rather than explicitly applied, within a space by the use of three-dimensional forms that, when tessellated, redefine our usual perception of surfaces such as wall and floor.

Historic, cultural connections and identities are reinforced by the juxtaposition of traditional and contemporary design.

Sophisticated articulation and textural opportunities through technological innovation on the walls and floors we design allow for light (and sometimes sound) to play on the surfaces that we often forget.

'The building becomes
an architectural adventure.'
OMA

Above:
**Casa da Musica, Rotunda
da Boavista, Porto, Portugal,
OMA, 2005**
The VIP area of this concert
hall combines traditional,
hand-painted Portuguese
tiles depicting pastoral
scenes, with contemporary,
corrugated glazing.

Facing page:
**James Cameron store,
Melbourne, Australia,
by Universal Design Studio,
2009**
The repetition of archive boxes
gives a gridded effect to a wall.

At the start of this chapter we considered the generally understood perception of tiles as small, hard, pieces of ceramic that combine to form a larger design. As we draw towards the end, we have the chance to consider projects where designers have challenged these perceptions and created the effect of tiles but in materials (both two dimensional and three dimensional) that one would not normally expect. This results in what we would often consider insignificant surfaces being brought forward and taking on a greater role in the performance and narrative of the interior.

Dreamtime Australia Design

Name:
Victor Churchill Butchery

Location:
Sydney, Australia

Date:
2009

Designer:
Dreamtime Australia Design

Modelled on a traditional European butchery but combined with innovative design elements, Victor Churchill have combined pride in their trade with an interior that evokes all the qualities and sensory experience of their produce: sandstone walls; copper and glass shelving; timber panelling; Italian marble floors and leather wall cladding to act as a stage on which the staff perform. A backdrop of a gently illuminated Himalayan rock-salt wall not only echoes the curing of meat and infuses it with flavour, but also helps to sterilize the air.

Above:
Blocks of Himalayan rock-salt are tiled to create a wall that helps to cure meat and sterilize the air.

> '"Clouds" coats architecture in a fluid yet chaotic way; bringing surprisingly colourful fabric windows to your place.'

Ronan and Erwan Bouroullec

Ronan and Erwan Bouroullec

Name:
'Clouds', with Kvadrat

Location:
N/A

Date:
2008

Designer:
Ronan and Erwan Bouroullec

'Clouds' uses an innovative tile made from a single, flexible, textile element that can be joined in any combination using the special rubber-band fixings. Designed by the Bouroullec brothers, this product is intended to be assembled into either two-dimensional forms that can be hung from the walls or the ceiling or three-dimensional forms that can stand freely in space. The simplicity of the design allows you to arrange and rearrange the tiles and express your creativity and ideas.

Above:
The tile elements are made from a single flexible textile.

Right:
A two-dimensional installation hanging from a wall.

It is difficult to consider the usual definitions of sustainable and ecological issues when one thinks of the huge variety of materials that have been and are being used as tiles. Just in the brief selection presented in this chapter, it is clear that both traditional and contemporary design have appropriated the idea of the tile and made it work with just about any material you care to think of.

The sustainability, or otherwise, of any tile must be considered with the ecological and environmental issues that surround the source material: ceramics are often clay-based products that need to be thought of in the same vein as brick. Concrete and stone tiles carry the same environmental impact as all stone and concrete products and plastics, glass, composite and metal tiles should all be considered on their ecological merit.

Where the idea of the tile can contribute to the debate is in the amount of material that it uses. We have seen in previous chapters how expensive materials such as stone have moved away from their traditional construction methods and developed into materials that act as cladding over a frame; the design often intended to give the appearance of solidity and mass, in contrast to the reality. If we re-evaluate the concept of the tile, as have many of the contemporary designs illustrated here, then we can use exotic and expensive materials in thinner, smaller, cheaper and more efficient modules as a covering to mundane substructures; thereby maintaining the opportunities for creativity as well as allowing for greater sustainability.

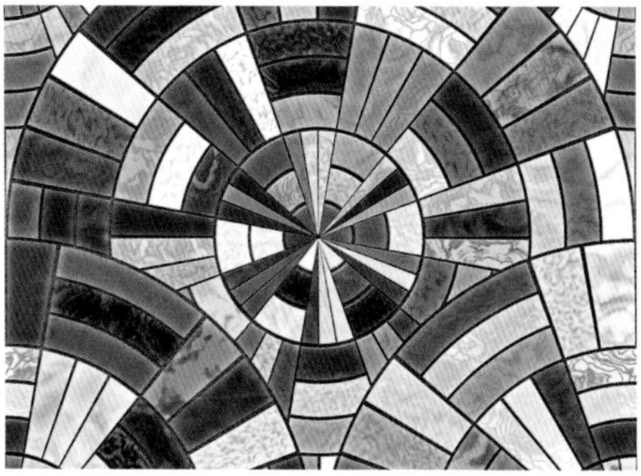
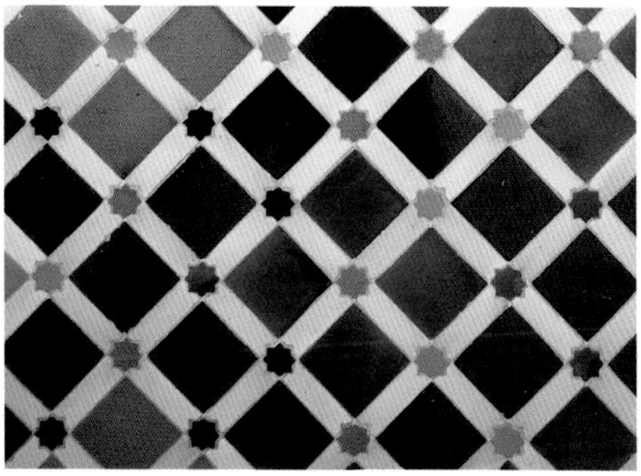
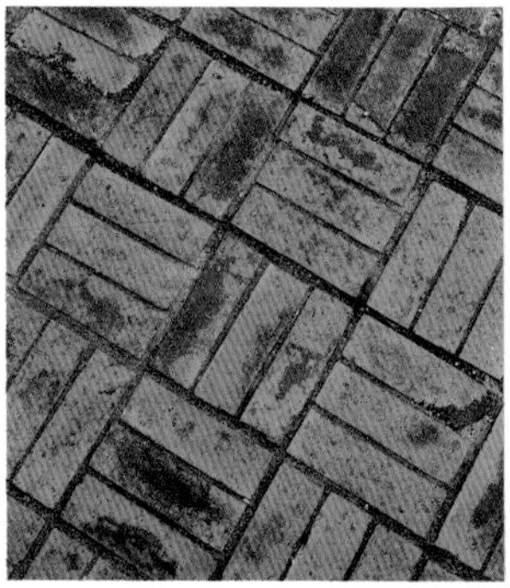
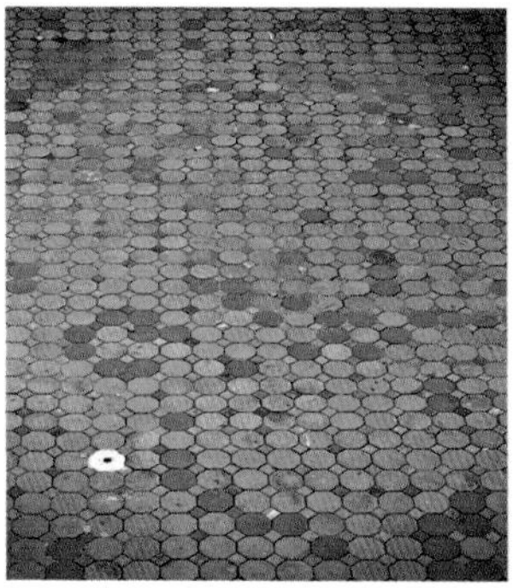
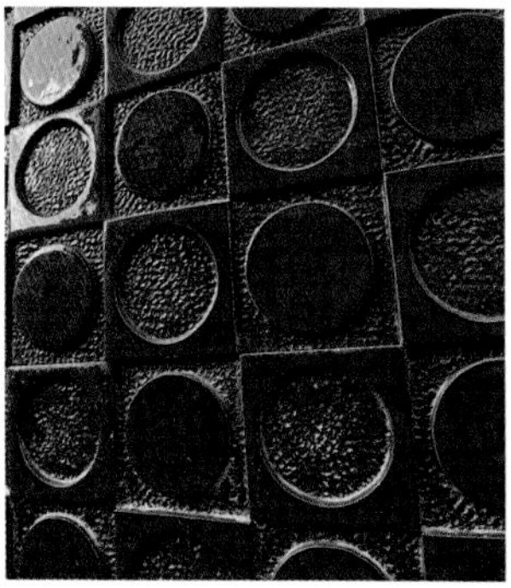
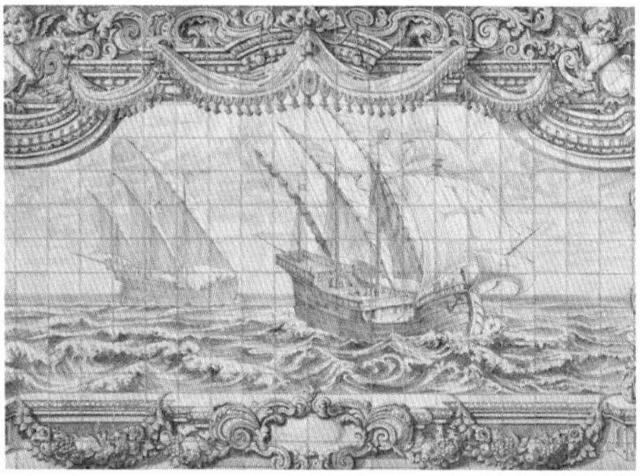
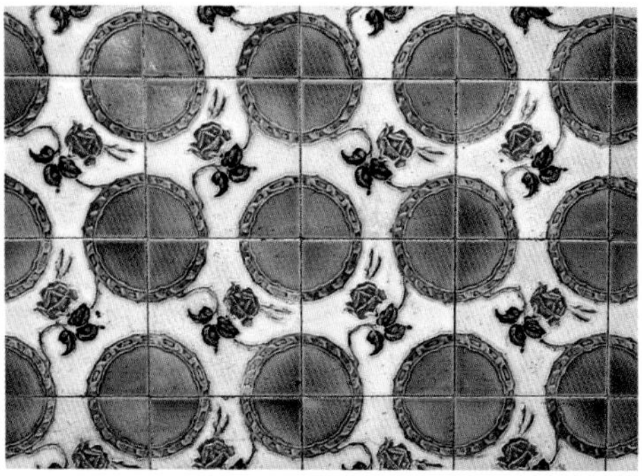
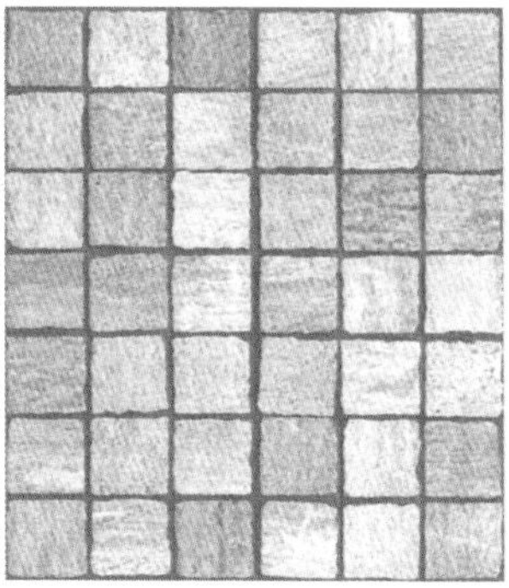
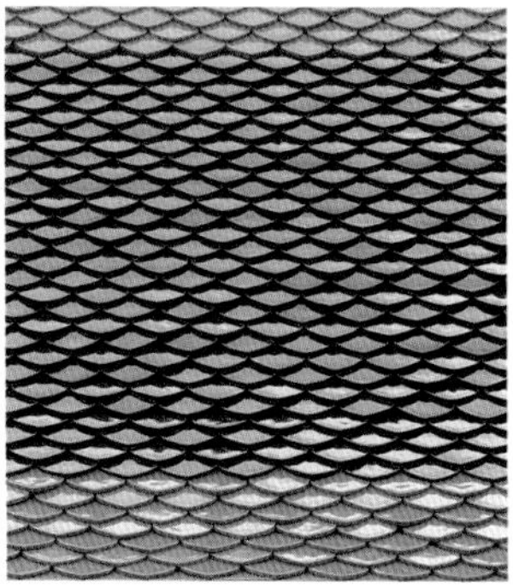
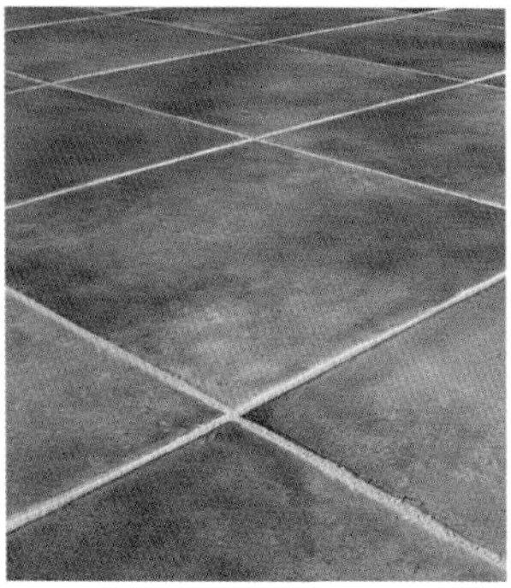

Tiles have been used for thousands of years to apply a durable and often richly ornamented surface to our interior spaces. Whilst the range of materials used to create tiles and a tiled effect has changed little in most of that time, more recent developments have propelled tiles to the forefront of innovative, contemporary design. Moving beyond the purely perceived decorative finish to a level of functionality that in itself becomes an aesthetic statement, the disrupted, modular, repetitive surface is having a real effect on the experience of interior space.

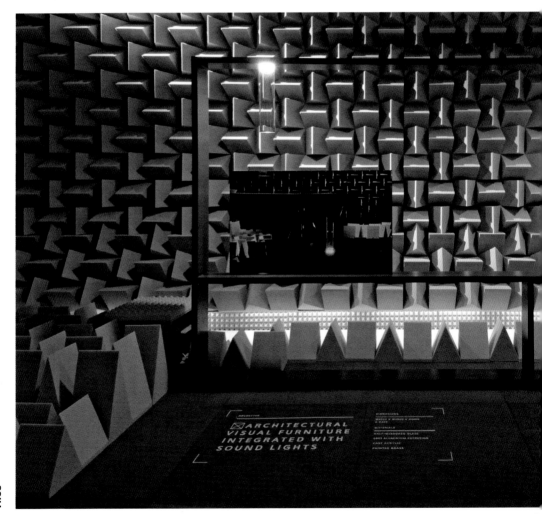

Contemplating Monolithic Design exhibition

Name:
'Contemplating
Monolithic Design'

Location:
Milan, Italy

Date:
2010

Designer:
Sony and Barber Osgerby

Today, with the huge variety
of materials that are being
modelled as tiles, designers
are experimenting with the
opportunities that the breaking
down of previously continuous
interior surfaces can bring
to the performance of those
spaces. The visual and
acoustic qualities of a space –
so important to be able to
optimize and, until recently,
so difficult to control – have
used the advantages that the
repetition and ordering of
these smaller elements bring.

In 2010, designers Barber
Osgerby teamed up with
Sony in an exhibition called
'Contemplating Monolithic
Design'. Sony wished to
demonstrate a range of products
that integrated approaches
to electronics, furniture and
architectural design. In order
to reveal the full experiential
effect of Sony's concepts,
Barber Osgerby constructed
an anechoic chamber, tiled with
hundreds of sound-absorbing
cones to create a noiseless
space: hearing becomes keener
and vision becomes sharper,
enabling the visitor to gain the
full range of experiences that
Sony intended.

Left:
The anechoic chamber,
tiled with hundreds of
sound-absorbing cones
to make a noiseless space.

Sustainability > **Innovations and the future**

Coatings and coverings

It might be thought, in a book looking at the materials and textures used in interior architecture that the wide variety of coatings and coverings should take priority over other chapters – interiors is all about wallpaper and paint is it not? Actually though, this book has shown that there are many materials that are now being used within our discipline to create the most inspiring of interior spaces and that, whatever the preconceptions of 'interiors' may be, those materials that cover and coat surfaces and objects are simply another opportunity for innovative design.

The application of one surface to another implies thinness of coating or covering, but this application can transform the impression and feeling of a space. Visual or real lack of weight in material should not be mistaken for lack of substance in effect.

The business of interior architecture is concerned with the design and communication of form and effect; the application of coatings and coverings can help visualize and emphasize effect and so successfully communicate the relationship between forms.

Name:
Soundwave Flo

Location:
N/A

Date:
2009

Designer:
Karim Rashid

These acoustic control panels are made of recycled, moulded, polyester fibre panels, designed to control higher frequency sounds such as voices and telephones.

The early use of plaster, or stucco, made of lime, to coat the surfaces of buildings has been recorded as far back as 3000 BC. An easily mouldable material able to take impressions and designs before drying as hard as stone, forms of plasterwork have allowed societies to adorn and ornament their buildings ever since.

For thousands of years, imagery, like so many forms of decoration, was restricted to religious, mythological and symbolic representation, but as grand buildings became designed for more secular reasons, the use of plasterwork also became more artistic and decorative.

Throughout the Renaissance, baroque and rococo movements, as we have seen with other materials in this book, plaster (often painted or gilded) was used to coat and embellish rooms. Surfaces, structures and the junctions between them became so elaborate that they seem to dissolve; the skill of the craftsman in producing such ornate mouldings demonstrated the wealth of the patron.

Facing page:
Interior of the Munich Residence, Munich, Germany, 1385
The former residence of the Bavarian monarchs is now an art museum. The use of gilt, and of mirrors, brings both a real and perceived lightness to the grandest of rooms.

Below:
Mayan wall murals, Bonampak, Mexico, AD 500
The Mayans created stuccos often depicting court rituals and human sacrifice.

Gilding

Briefly mentioned above is the idea of gilding – the process of applying gold leaf or powder to a solid surface. The use of plasterwork in the interior allowed for large areas of flat wall, or bulky structural elements, to be visually broken down by increasingly more elaborate decorative effects.

Along with a greater degree of decoration in the interior also came the greater use of light. As the manufacture of glass developed, the wealthy could increase the areas of windows in their buildings. Gold leaf on the relief forms created by plasterwork caught the light (both natural and from candles), and could make the interior shimmer and sparkle. Interestingly, in an age of poor artificial light (good candles being expensive and gas lamps not in common use until the nineteenth century), the glint and shine of details picked out in gold could also help the occupants find their way safely to bed!

Left:
**The General Assembly
hall of the United Nations,
New York, USA, by
Wallace K Harrison,
1949**
The large expanse of gold leaf
behind the president's platform
not only provides a dramatic
and glittering backdrop to the
proceedings but also connects
with historic ideas of power,
authority and prestige.

**Facing page:
The JS Bach Chamber
Music Hall, Manchester, UK,
by Zaha Hadid Architects,
2009**
A translucent fabric membrane
tensioned over an internal steel
structure provides auditorium,
performance space and control
of light and sound.

Textile coverings

The idea of covering the walls of a space
with a heavy tapestry or cloth (to provide
a sense of warmth and comfort) was
common practice from medieval times.
This developed through the early sixteenth
and seventeenth centuries, most notably
with the Chinese print and paint designs,
typically of birds, flowers and landscapes,
on sheets of rice paper or lengths of silk.
Whilst very expensive at the time, wall
coverings based around the application
of a luxurious material or design has
never really gone out of fashion – and the
opportunity to follow fashion, by simply
changing the covering of your walls, has
proven to be attractive to both designers
and clients ever since.

In contemporary design, fabrics, textiles,
coatings and coverings have been used
to produce lightweight, often temporary,
interior spaces and installations that make
full use of the traditional opportunities
that these materials give to control and
modulate light, change the nature of space
and create space itself.

Coatings and Coverings

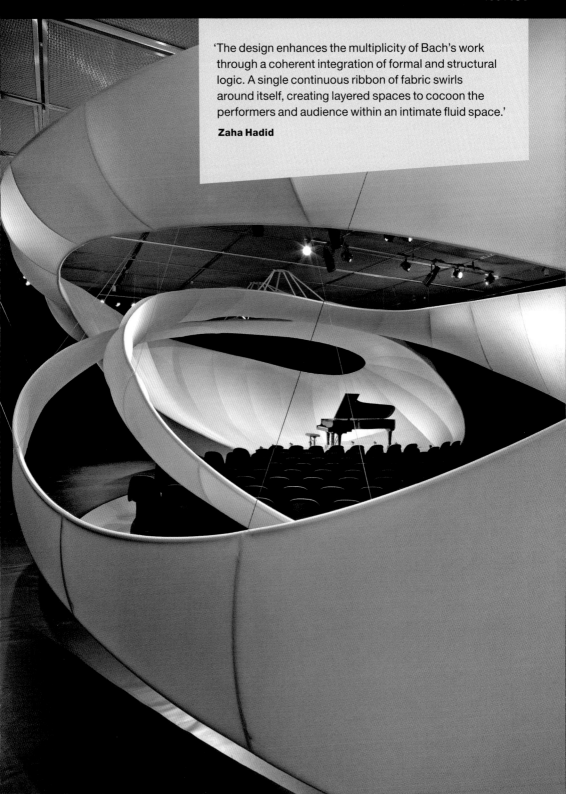

'The design enhances the multiplicity of Bach's work through a coherent integration of formal and structural logic. A single continuous ribbon of fabric swirls around itself, creating layered spaces to cocoon the performers and audience within an intimate fluid space.'

Zaha Hadid

The preceding section of this chapter has looked at those materials that have been used to coat and cover surfaces in the more conventional sense of the design of the interior; the accentuation of form and the enhancement of effect being the primary goals of their application. In this section we will look at how contemporary design is using coatings and coverings on surfaces and objects in order to further drive the design and communication of form and effect, whilst taking into consideration aspects such as function, experience and aesthetics.

Function

In the Chamber Music Hall by Hadid we saw how a material has been used to both create space and control sound. The control of sound by the use of another material within a space has long been understood. Even in the auditoria of the eighteenth century, the traditional horseshoe shape and soft furnishings were used to both focus the sound (and view) coming from the stage and to control the unwanted reverberation and reflection of sound around the space. Today, acoustic design has developed into a sophisticated science where the form of the space, the design of the fittings and furnishings and even the occupation of the audience and performers all have an impact on how space is controlled – both from within and without.

Sound-absorbing and sound-reducing techniques have not escaped the notice of interior design and the opportunity such materials give to create surface forms and unusual textural effects that are at the same time luxurious, ornamental and functional.

Such uses can often result in some of the most stark and disturbing of interior spaces – spaces that exist as much for their psychological effect as their functional efficiency.

**Facing page:
Underground shelter,
Emigrant, Montana, USA,
Charlie Hull, 2003**
Built for post-apocalypse shelter, this subterranean and steel-lined shelter tries to combine the 'comforts' of home in a scenario that few of us would wish to imagine; the functional needs of the structure describe a disturbing yet strangely beautiful space.

Experience

Every interior space should create an experience for the user – that is what we all hope to achieve as designers. As we have seen in the historical section of this chapter, the use of coatings and coverings such as stucco, gilding and fabrics dramatically change the feel and impression of a space with relatively little effort. In today's drive for short turnaround times and value for money, designers often make use of low-budget but high-drama effects in their designs.

Taking the experiential to, perhaps, its logical conclusion, designers are using technology to experiment with the virtual coating of space using images that are not only constantly changing but which are also generated by ourselves and the lives that we lead.

Above and facing page: SPRMRKT STH retail store, Amsterdam, Netherlands, by Doepel Strijkers Architects, 2010
Intended to bring skin, body and clothing together, a tensile fabric stretched over a structure of mannequins creates a second skin within the store. Emphasizing both perfection and imperfection, the fabric is tensioned and torn to both create and reveal space.

Coatings and Coverings

'We were inspired by perfection versus imperfection and driven by bodily irregularities, such as the mutation of skin through tattoos and piercings. The human body can be seen as a form of clothing that conveys personality. We wanted to bring skin, body and clothing together, but in a subtle way.'

**Eline Strijkers of
Doepel Strijkers Architects**

Below:
**DATAMATICS at the Ars
Electronica Centre, Linz,
Austria, by Ryoji Ikeda, 2010**
Eight DLP projectors, computers,
9.2ch sound system were used
to create this art project, which
explores the potential to perceive
the invisible multi-substance
of data that permeates our world.

Aesthetics

As we have seen from some of the previous examples, not all the spaces making use of coated or covered surfaces could be described as 'aesthetically pleasing', but those that are not are intentionally not – as designers, we should always make our intentions clear and deliberate. Sometimes the use of one surface to coat or cover another can result in a beautiful, aesthetic effect that does bring delight to our interior.

The coating of surfaces can even take place on a molecular level, but as noted at the very start of this chapter, the visual or real lack of weight in material should not be mistaken for lack of substance in effect.

Deliberate use of the word appropriation has been made in the title of this section. Many of the projects considered earlier are in themselves both innovative and exemplars of their type. It is hoped that this section will show how coatings and coverings that have a direct historic precedent have been appropriated by contemporary designers and transformed into works that demonstrate leading-edge design.

RGB Wallpaper

Name:
RGB wallpaper

Location:
N/A

Date:
2010

Designer:
Carnovsky

Looking at images of natural history between the sixteenth and nineteenth centuries, Carnovsky conjure up images of both the factual and the fantastic. Calibrating the colour of the prints to that of the filters through which the panels are viewed, the designers succeed in drawing out different layers of imagery for the viewer. Red light exposes the cyan of the reptiles and the birds; yellow insects crawl out under a blue light only to recede when the light turns white.

Transforming the static, two-dimensional nature of wallpaper into something dynamic and changing, Francesco Rugi and Silvia Quintanilla have succeeded in both exploring and creating real and perceived depth, a 'surface deepness', from the most ubiquitous of coverings.

Left:
'RGB Wallpaper'
Three different images, each one in a primary colour, are superimposed on one another using a transparent material. The resultant overlapping and intertwined image produces a three-dimensional effect on a two-dimensional surface.

Kokon furniture

Name:
Kokon furniture

Location:
N/A

Date:
1999

Designer:
Makkink & Bey

Using textiles to cover surfaces within the interior has probably been in practice since man started to occupy his own space. Architect Rianne Makkink and designer Jurgen Bey have subverted this concept by taking a contemporary textile and shrink-wrapping the objects that occupy our spaces. Working to a fundamental philosophy of 'cross-wiring' between different areas of expertise – and an undeniable sense of fun and exploration – Makkink and Bey have taken the very familiar, the banal and obsolete, and given them a new lease of life. The furniture that provides the underlying structure to their elastic fibre is still both recognizable and functional, but the blurring of the boundaries between individual objects, giving the appearance that one is almost growing out of the other, takes the familiar out of context, confusing identity and creating new and disturbing forms.

Above:
'Kokon furniture and panel'
A combination of objects and furniture are effectively shrink-wrapped by an elastic, synthetic fibre creating a smooth skin that radically changes their appearance.

Coatings and Coverings

Touchy Feely tiles

Name:
Touchy Feely

Location:
N/A

Date:
2006

Designer:
Stephanie Davidson and
Georg Rafailidis

Touchy Feely Haptic Design was intended to create a 'sensory conversation', a more heightened sensory experience between the body and the built environment. Key to the designers' philosophy is humour, curiosity, an experimental approach to materials, an interest in incidental design, and more physical interaction with the built environment. Making prototypes of their designs is an integral part of the design process, the interaction of the body often directly generating the forms of their design.

A surface such as plaster, so long used to cover the basic materials of wall construction that it too has almost become invisible, is reworked here in both form and function to provide a three-dimensional surface that also works with the body that so often moves against it.

Above:
'Trigger Points' plaster mouldings in fibre-reinforced plaster
The plaster mouldings incorporate a heating element to allow a degree of massage and comfort as people interact with the forms.

Like so many of the materials considered in this book, questions of sustainability are controversial and depend largely on your view of sustainable use as well as the material of your choice. This chapter has only touched on the large range of materials available to the interior architect with which surfaces and objects can be either covered or coated. Issues of appropriate ecological or environmental use are as varied as the range of materials.

Paint producers are now having to reconsider the solvents used in their manufacturing processes as well as the odours produced when the products are applied; plaster is now available with additives that reflect heat back into your room and so aid in insulation and the reduction of heat loss through your walls; textiles such as soft furnishings, carpets and flooring are now being made of natural, sustainable, biodegradable materials such as hemp, sisal and bamboo. In short, whilst there is no overarching approach to the environmental and ecological agenda, many of the more familiar coatings and coverings used in the interior are looking to employ a greater awareness and responsible attitude to their make-up and manufacture. Such approaches do not limit our choices as designers but rather open up new possibilities and opportunities for innovative design and offer the choice of moving away from many of the 'unecological' and environmentally unfriendly materials of past years.

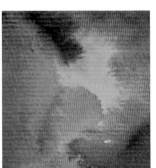

Innovative appropriation > **Sustainability**

Conclusion

The aim of this book, as mentioned at the start, was not to present definitive, glossy examples of materials and their use but to engage the student designer in questioning where, when, how and why a material should, or could, be used. Here, at the end, it is worth considering whether those aims have been achieved.

Your choice and use of materials can make or break a design. Interior architecture is concerned with the communication of form and effect within spaces. The correct use of materials and textures can dramatically accentuate form and enhance effect but it is perhaps inappropriate to use terms such as 'correct use'. What we have seen throughout this book is that the design of interior spaces, through history, has progressed and developed and thrown up something new and dynamic when designers have chosen to experiment and break established rules and conventions: the aesthetic movements developed as a direct reaction to the perceived excesses of the Victorian era; modernism developed in reaction to the obsession with craft and in response to the demands and opportunities of the industrial age and contemporary design has progressed hand-in-hand with technological, manufacturing, economic and social achievements.

Today, as has hopefully been shown in this book, you have an unparalleled opportunity to break the rules, to make use of an ever-increasing range of materials in an ever-increasing range of interior applications. As society has changed so have the types of spaces that you will be called upon to design but so have the ethical responsibilities of the designer. The materials that you choose to specify to create and enhance your spaces always come at a cost. With the globalization of design, that cost is also global: ecological, social and economic. I have hoped not to convey any judgement on the use of materials in the case-studies shown here but it is vital that as you develop as designers you consider the impact of the choices that you make. The responsibilities that are placed on you as designers should not be seen as limitations, rather as opportunities to be experimental, dynamic, creative and innovative – rising to this challenge is what will mark you out as being above the average, as being exceptional.

Aesthetic The appreciation of beauty; in this context referring to an artistic movement of the mid-nineteenth century that believed in 'art for art's sake' and rejected the notion that art should have a deeper social or moral purpose.

Anechoic A space that is free from echo and is used to absorb or deaden sound.

Anodising An electrolytic process that coats a metal (usually aluminium) with a protective oxide layer. This process not only protects the metal from oxidization but can also apply colour.

Art Deco A fashion-orientated style of the 1920s and 1930s characterized by the use of rich materials such as marble, aluminium, black glass, lacquer and gilt in geometric and cubist forms.

Art Nouveau Late-nineteenth-century style characterized by the artistic and naturalistic appropriation of modern materials (such as iron, glass and wood) and the rejection of the Victorian obsession with imitation.

Arts and Crafts (the aesthetic movements) A style adopted at the end of the nineteenth and start of the twentieth centuries that typically reacted to the excesses of the Victorian and championed the work of the craftsman.

Baroque An essentially European style of design that followed the High Renaissance of the sixteenth century. Generally restricted to religious buildings, the style was characterized by an emphasis on sculptural, naturalistic and painted forms.

Buttress Stone or brick that is built against a wall in order to provide additional support.

Cast iron Iron forms that have been created by the pouring of the molten metal into a mould. Such a technique allowed for the consistent reproduction of structural elements and ornament.

Classical orders (of architecture) Usually considered to be Doric, Ionic and Corinthian. Principles of design, such as proportion, style and ornamentation, influenced by the work of the ancient Greeks and Romans.

Classical revival Late eighteenth and early nineteenth century period of adoption and amalgamation of the styles of ancient Greece and Rome.

Clerestory Usually referring to the upper area of the nave or choir in a church which contains windows.

Column An upright pillar that supports an opening, an arch or other structural element of a building; a column can also stand in isolation as a monumental element.

'Cradle to cradle' Often shown as 'C2C' or 'Cradle2Cradle'. A holistic, economic, industrial and social approach to design and resource use that seeks to create systems and processes that are efficient and waste-free.

'Cradle to grave' A technique devised to assess the environmental impact of a product from its inception to its disposal.

Ductility The ability of metal to be drawn into a thin wire.

Engineered wood Wood that is made up of other elements, such as plywood, where thin layers of wood are laminated, with alternate grain direction, using adhesives. The result is often a product that is lighter, stronger and more resistant to chemical and biological attack than natural wood.

Gilding To cover a surface with a thin layer of a precious metal, most commonly gold but also silver and copper.

Gothic A term that was originally used pejoratively to describe the architecture of the Middle Ages. Later, with the construction of increasingly skilled and elaborate buildings, it became used to describe a definitive style, often evident in religious buildings. The Gothic style was revived and elaborated in the nineteenth century.

Gravity construction (also known as 'mass construction') When materials that are used in construction (such as stone and brick) are kept in place by the action of gravity transferring the loads that are applied to them down to the ground.

Haptic Relating to the sense of touch.

Keystone The final central stone of an arch that applies compressive force to voussoirs on either side.

Lintel A horizontal support across an opening (such as a door or window or between columns as common in the architecture of ancient Greece).

Mannerist / Mannerism Characterizing a personally expressive style adopted by some artists during the Renaissance as a reaction to the accepted ways of working.

Marquetry Inlaid work made from small pieces a coloured and highly-figured woods.

Mason Someone who builds or works with stone. Until the fifteenth century the designers and makers of buildings were one and the same people – craftsmen and artisans (the carpenter and the mason) who had learned their trades over generations and were experts at translating the wishes of their patrons into built forms. Very little was drawn or modelled, the patron instead relying on the inherent knowledge of the craftsman. The designer didn't exist.

Modernism Progressive movement at the start of the twentieth century that connected itself with the 'machine age', the products of industry, mass production and the rejection of ornament.

Moorish Typically making reference in early Christian buildings (eleventh and twelfth centuries) to influences from North Africa of around the eighth century.

Parquetry Similar to marquetry but characterized by the use of geometric patterns.

Patina Any distinctive surface (colour or texture) acquired on a material (usually wood or metal) over time.

Pilaster A rectangular column often projecting from a wall.

Postmodernism A theoretical basis to design first put forward by the architect Robert Venturi in his book *Complexity and Contradiction in Architecture* (1966) in which he calls for the strictures and limitations of modernism to be put aside in favour of a greater complexity to design, bringing it it closer connection to human qualities.

Renaissance A gradual move away from the thinking of the medieval period that is generally considered to have started in Italy around 1400 and moved through Europe until around the late sixteenth century.

Rococo Generally seen as a further, more refined, development of the Baroque that was primarily used in secular buildings of the eighteenth century.

Streamlined design Mid-twentieth century, predominantly American, style drawing inspiration from speed, transport, industry and industrial products. Most clearly demonstrated in the American diner interiors of the 1940s and 1950s.

Sustainability As a result of the 1987 United Nations Brundtland Report, an accepted definition of sustainability has become familiar to us: sustainable development is development that meets the needs of the present without compromising the ability of future generations to meet their own needs. This statement was further reinforced by the Outcome Document of the United Nations 2005 World Summit which stated that the 'interdependent and mutually reinforcing pillars' of sustainable development should be considered as economic development, social development, and environmental protection.

Tessellation The repeated use of a single shape without gaps or overlapping, most commonly evident in the use of tiles and mosaics.

Vault roof A roof in the form of an arch or series of arches.

Voussoir A wedge-shaped or tapered stone used to construct an arch and kept in place by the compressive force applied by the keystone.

Wrought iron Iron given form and texture by working, such as hammering and bending.

The following lists some of the designers, studios and manufacturers that have inspired the writing of this book.

A-Asterisk Design
China
www.a-asterisk.com

Agence Andrée Putman
France
www.studioputman.com/english/index.html

Ball Nogues Studio
USA
www.ball-nogues.com

Brinkworth
UK
www.brinkworth.co.uk

Carnovsky
Italy
www.carnovsky.com

Caruso St John Architects
UK
www.carusostjohn.com

Clive Wilkinson Architects
USA and UK
www.clivewilkinson.com

Cox Architecture
Australia
www.coxarchitecture.com.au

Dale Chihuly, Artist
USA
www.chihuly.com

de Gournay Ltd
UK
www.degournay.com

Doepel Strijkers Architects
Netherlands
www.dsarotterdam.com

Dreamtime Australian Design
Australia
www.dreamtimeaustraliadesign.com

Elding Oscarson
Sweden
www.eldingoscarson.com

Erwin Hauer
USA
www.erwinhauer.com

Eva Jiricna Architects
UK
www.ejal.com

Gore Design Co. Arizona
USA
www.goredesignco.com

Greg Lynn Architect
www.glform.com

Iwan Halstead and Emily Rickards
UK
www.daytripstudio.com

John Pawson Ltd
UK
www.johnpawson.com

John Robertson Architects
UK
www.jra.co.uk

Jurgen Mayer H
Germany
www.jmayerh.de

Karim Rashid
USA and Netherlands
www.karimrashid.com

Korban/Flaubert
Australia
www.korbanflaubert.com.au

Kriska Décor
curtain manufacturer
Spain
www.kriskadecor.com

Kvadrat Ltd
Denmark and International
www.kvadrat.dk

Maison Koichiro
Kimura & International
Japan
www.love-international.jp

Marc Fornes & Theverymany
USA
www.theverymany.com

Miniwiz Sustainable Energy Development Ltd
Taiwan
www.miniwiz.com

Project Import Export
USA
www.projectimportexport.com

Riccardo Giovanetti Design
Italy
www.riccardogiovanetti.it

Ron Arad Associates
UK
www.ronarad.co.uk

Ronan and Erwan Bouroullec
France
www.bouroullec.com

Ryoji Ikeda
Composer and installation artist
Japan
www.ryojikeda.com

Shizuka Hariu & Shin Bogdan Hagiwara
Architecture + Scenography
Belgium, UK and Japan
www.shsh.be

SIC Arquitectura y Urbanismo
Spain
www.estudiofam.com

Snøhetta Architects
Norway
www.snohetta.com

Studio Fuksas
Italy
www.fuksas.it

Studio Makkink and Bey Design Studio
Netherlands
www.studiomakkinkbey.nl

Swarovski
www.architecture.swarovski.com

Tom Dixon Design Research Studio
UK
www.designresearchstudio.net

Thomas Heatherwick Heatherwick Studio
UK
www.heatherwick.com

Touchy Feely Haptic Design
Germany
www.touchy-feely.net

Universal Design Studio
UK and Australia
www.universaldesignstudio.com

Weitzner Ltd
USA
www.weitznerlimited.com

Zaha Hadid Architects
UK
www.zaha-hadid.com

Compiled by Indexing Specialists
(UK) Ltd

Acknowledgements

First of all my sincere thanks and appreciation must to go all my colleagues at the Arts University College, Bournemouth and to the students and graduates of BA (Hons) Interior Architecture and Design for their help, support and encouragement during the writing of this book. Their combined knowledge, skill, hard work and excellence in educating have been invaluable.

A huge debt of appreciation also goes to all those designers, studios, organizations and individuals who continue to support the education of interior architects and interior designers and have generously contributed to this book.

A special mention to Leafy Cummins at AVA for her encouragement, patience and support and without whom none of this would have had any chance of happening. Thanks also to Maeliosa O'Brien, Michele Thompson and Jean Whitehead for their help with reviewing early manuscripts and proposals.

Lastly to Gemma, Isaac and Oscar – without your constant enthusiasm, humour, support, encouragement and love (and copious supplies of late-night coffee) I would not be writing this now. Thank you.

Cover image and 158:
Design: Carnovsky.
Photo: Alvise Vivenza
002: Photograph by
Shuhei Kaihara
009: Karim Rashid Inc.
012: Tadao Ando
020: Simon Hadleigh –
Sparks/Syon House
027: Graeme Brooker
028: Courtesy of Caruso St John
029: Courtesy of Caruso St John
032: © ARTEDIA/VIEW
033: Weinerchaise brick chair
by Andy Martin Associates
at 100% Design. Image courtesy
of 100% Design.
041: Photograph by Paul Gosney
042: Max Alexander
044: Heatherwick Studio
045: © Nathan Willock/VIEW
048: © David Borland/VIEW
057: The amazing roof of 3 slip
© Chatham Historic
Dockyard Trust
058: RIBA Library
Photographs Collection
059: RIBA Library
Photographs Collection
060: David Borland/VIEW
062+063: Graeme Brooker
064+065: Photographs by
Iwan Baan
068: David Linley
069: Courtesy of the
artist/designer
070: Photo by Terry Rishel
© Chihuly Studio
080+081: Steve Speller
081: Drawing courtesy
of Heatherwick Studio
082+083: Graeme Brooker
087: © Swarovski AG2011.
All rights reserved
088: Drawings courtesy of
Zaha Hadid Architects
089: Hélène Binet
090: Ball-Nogues Studio
092: Architectural Press Archive/
RIBA Library Photographs
Collection

095: © Ateliers Jean Nouvel.
Photograph by Fotoworks
098: Karim Rashid Inc.
100+101: © Hufton + Crow/
VIEW
102+103: Karim Rashid Inc.
104+105: Studio Bouroullec et
Tahon et Bouroullec
108+109: Studio Giovanetti
110: Doriana and
Massimiliano Fuksas.
Photograph © Ramon Prat
114: Ron Arad
116: Photograph by
Shuhei Kaihara
118+119: Erwin Hauer
120+121: Courtesy of
Zaha Hadid Architects
124: Photography by
Jake Fitzjones for DuPont,
all rights reserved. Design by
Brinkworth for Fortnum & Mason,
Fabrication by Cutting Edge
125: Marc Fornes
126: Architect: Elding Oscarson,
Photographer: Åke Eson Lindman
133: © Victoria & Albert Museum,
London
135: Bargain Betty
136: Koichiro Kimura
137: Courtesy of
Studio Makkink & Bey BV
138: Scottie Cameron
139: © Carlos Coutinho.
All rights reserved
140: Photograph by Paul Gosney
141: Studio Bouroullec et
Tahon et Bouroullec
144: Courtesy of Sony Design
146: Karim Rashid Inc.
151: © Luke Hayes/VIEW
153: © Richard Ross
154: Design: Doepel Strijkers
Architects. Photography:
Wouter vandenBrink
156: Liz Hingley
www.lizhingley.com
160: Jurgen Bey/Dry-tech/
Collection Droog. Design/photo:
Bob Goedewaagen/1999
Courtesy of Droog Design
161: Georg Rafailidis

All reasonable attempts have
been made to trace, clear and
credit the copyright holders of the
images reproduced in this book.
However, if any credits have been
inadvertently omitted, the
publisher will endeavour to
incorporate amendments in
future editions.

Publisher's note

The subject of ethics is not new, yet its consideration within the applied visual arts is perhaps not as prevalent as it might be. Our aim here is to help a new generation of students, educators and practitioners find a methodology for structuring their thoughts and reflections in this vital area.

AVA Publishing hopes that these **Working with ethics** pages provide a platform for consideration and a flexible method for incorporating ethical concerns in the work of educators, students and professionals. Our approach consists of four parts:

The **introduction** is intended to be an accessible snapshot of the ethical landscape, both in terms of historical development and current dominant themes.

The **framework** positions ethical consideration into four areas and poses questions about the practical implications that might occur. Marking your response to each of these questions on the scale shown will allow your reactions to be further explored by comparison.

The **case study** sets out a real project and then poses some ethical questions for further consideration. This is a focus point for a debate rather than a critical analysis so there are no predetermined right or wrong answers.

A selection of **further reading** for you to consider areas of particular interest in more detail.

Ethical: awareness/ reflection/ debate

Working with ethics

Introduction

Ethics is a complex subject that interlaces the idea of responsibilities to society with a wide range of considerations relevant to the character and happiness of the individual. It concerns virtues of compassion, loyalty and strength, but also of confidence, imagination, humour and optimism. As introduced in ancient Greek philosophy, the fundamental ethical question is: *what should I do?* How we might pursue a 'good' life not only raises moral concerns about the effects of our actions on others, but also personal concerns about our own integrity.

In modern times the most important and controversial questions in ethics have been the moral ones. With growing populations and improvements in mobility and communications, it is not surprising that considerations about how to structure our lives together on the planet should come to the forefront. For visual artists and communicators, it should be no surprise that these considerations will enter into the creative process.

Some ethical considerations are already enshrined in government laws and regulations or in professional codes of conduct. For example, plagiarism and breaches of confidentiality can be punishable offences. Legislation in various nations makes it unlawful to exclude people with disabilities from accessing information or spaces. The trade of ivory as a material has been banned in many countries. In these cases, a clear line has been drawn under what is unacceptable.

But most ethical matters remain open to debate, among experts and lay-people alike, and in the end we have to make our own choices on the basis of our own guiding principles or values. Is it more ethical to work for a charity than for a commercial company? Is it unethical to create something that others find ugly or offensive?

Specific questions such as these may lead to other questions that are more abstract. For example, is it only effects on humans (and what they care about) that are important, or might effects on the natural world require attention too?

Is promoting ethical consequences justified even when it requires ethical sacrifices along the way? Must there be a single unifying theory of ethics (such as the Utilitarian thesis that the right course of action is always the one that leads to the greatest happiness of the greatest number), or might there always be many different ethical values that pull a person in various directions?

As we enter into ethical debate and engage with these dilemmas on a personal and professional level, we may change our views or change our view of others. The real test though is whether, as we reflect on these matters, we change the way we act as well as the way we think. Socrates, the 'father' of philosophy, proposed that people will naturally do 'good' if they know what is right. But this point might only lead us to yet another question: *how do we know what is right?*

You
What are your ethical beliefs?

Central to everything you do will be your attitude to people and issues around you. For some people, their ethics are an active part of the decisions they make every day as a consumer, a voter or a working professional. Others may think about ethics very little and yet this does not automatically make them unethical. Personal beliefs, lifestyle, politics, nationality, religion, gender, class or education can all influence your ethical viewpoint.

Using the scale, where would you place yourself? What do you take into account to make your decision? Compare results with your friends or colleagues.

Your client
What are your terms?

Working relationships are central to whether ethics can be embedded into a project, and your conduct on a day-to-day basis is a demonstration of your professional ethics. The decision with the biggest impact is whom you choose to work with in the first place. Cigarette companies or arms traders are often-cited examples when talking about where a line might be drawn, but rarely are real situations so extreme. At what point might you turn down a project on ethical grounds and how much does the reality of having to earn a living affect your ability to choose?

Using the scale, where would you place a project? How does this compare to your personal ethical level?

01 02 03 04 05 06 07 08 09 10

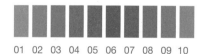

01 02 03 04 05 06 07 08 09 10

Your specifications
What are the impacts of your materials?

In relatively recent times, we are learning that many natural materials are in short supply. At the same time, we are increasingly aware that some man-made materials can have harmful, long-term effects on people or the planet. How much do you know about the materials that you use? Do you know where they come from, how far they travel and under what conditions they are obtained? When your creation is no longer needed, will it be easy and safe to recycle? Will it disappear without a trace? Are these considerations your responsibility or are they out of your hands?

Using the scale, mark how ethical your material choices are.

Your creation
What is the purpose of your work?

Between you, your colleagues and an agreed brief, what will your creation achieve? What purpose will it have in society and will it make a positive contribution? Should your work result in more than commercial success or industry awards? Might your creation help save lives, educate, protect or inspire? Form and function are two established aspects of judging a creation, but there is little consensus on the obligations of visual artists and communicators toward society, or the role they might have in solving social or environmental problems. If you want recognition for being the creator, how responsible are you for what you create and where might that responsibility end?

Using the scale, mark how ethical the purpose of your work is.

01 02 03 04 05 06 07 08 09 10

01 02 03 04 05 06 07 08 09 10

One aspect of interior architecture that can raise an ethical dilemma is the issue of creating interior spaces that may directly affect people's emotions or behaviours. This might be done in positive or negative ways and often leads to further questions about who benefits from the emotions or behaviours that are created. For example, commercial retail interiors can be designed to slow people down and encourage them to follow certain paths in order to increase the chance of them making purchases; or a commercial office interior may be designed to improve productivity. At what point should (or do) projects such as these take into account the needs of the consumer or the worker? Is it the responsibility of the interior architect to bear in mind the users, as well as the owners, of a space? Or are these considerations always in the hands of whoever funds the project?

Although London's Old Bailey has been rebuilt several times since 1674, the design of this courthouse remains largely the same. The accused stands in the dock directly facing the witness box and the judges are seated on the other side of the room. Jurors sit together so that they can consult with each other and arrive at their verdicts. Seated below the judges are clerks, lawyers and writers.

In 1673, the courtroom was opened on one side. This was done to increase the supply of fresh air to stop prisoners from spreading typhus. Spectators crowded into the outside yard and their presence could influence or intimidate the jurors sitting inside. In 1737, the building was remodelled and enclosed – not only to keep out the weather, but also to limit spectators. Consequently, an outbreak of typhus at one trial in 1750 led to the death of 60 people, including the Lord Mayor and two judges.

In 1774, the court was rebuilt with luxurious facilities for court personnel and a separate room was created for witnesses so that they would not have to wait at a nearby public house. A grand jury room contained 18 leather-seated chairs. Such lavish provision for the judges and their servants contrasted dramatically with the prisoners' quarters in the basement.

Before the introduction of gas lighting in the early-nineteenth century, a mirrored reflector was placed above the dock to reflect light onto the faces of the accused. This allowed the court to better examine facial expressions and assess their testimony. A sounding board was also placed over their heads in order to amplify their voices. In some courtrooms (those in which prisoners were still branded), the interior included irons for holding convicts' hands while they were burnt.

In 1877, it was decided to replace the courthouse with a larger building, which was finally opened by King Edward VII in 1907. Four oak-panelled courtrooms contained space for all those who needed to attend modern trials. There were now separate rooms for male and female witnesses, and another for witnesses of 'the better class'.

The Old Bailey was heavily damaged by bombing in 1941, but was subsequently rebuilt. A modern extension was added in 1972 but the current building, which is still England's most important crown court, remains essentially the same as the 1907 design.

Could the interior architecture of a courtroom affect the verdict?

Is it unethical to design an interior space to intimidate people?

Would you work on a courthouse project?

Rooms open into one another, everything communicates, and space is broken up into angles, diffuse areas and mobile sectors. Rooms, in short, have been liberalised.

Jean Baudrillard

AIGA
Design Business and Ethics
2007, AIGA

Eaton, Marcia Muelder
Aesthetics and the Good Life
1989, Associated University Press

Ellison, David
Ethics and Aesthetics in European Modernist Literature:
From the Sublime to the Uncanny
2001, Cambridge University Press

Fenner, David E W (Ed)
Ethics and the Arts:
An Anthology
1995, Garland Reference Library of Social Science

Gini, Al and Marcoux, Alexei M
Case Studies in Business Ethics
2005, Prentice Hall

McDonough, William and Braungart, Michael
Cradle to Cradle:
Remaking the Way We Make Things
2002, North Point Press

Papanek, Victor
Design for the Real World:
Making to Measure
1972, Thames & Hudson

United Nations Global Compact
The Ten Principles
www.unglobalcompact.org/AboutTheGC/TheTenPrinciples/index.html